First Edition
13 12 11   5 4 3 2

Copyright © 2010 JRL Publications

Created by:	Jeanette R. Lynton
Executive Director:	Kristine Widtfeldt
Creative Manager:	Kristy McDonnell
Art Director:	Eric Clegg
Contributing Writer:	Nicole Snow
Design:	Tracy O'Very Covey
Photography:	BPD Studios

Thanks to all the talented staff at Close To My Heart who
helped make this wonderful book come together.

Published by
Gibbs Smith
P.O. Box 667
Layton, Utah 84041

1-800-835-4993 Orders
www.gibbs-smith.com

Gibbs Smith books are printed on paper produced from
sustainable PEFC-certified forest/controlled wood source.
Learn more at: www.pefc.org
Printed and bound in Hong Kong

Library of Congress Control Number: 2010921967
ISBN 13: 978-1-4236-0439-6
ISBN 10: 1-4236-0439-3

Magic™

INTERACTIVE SCRAPBOOKS
THAT DAZZLE AND DELIGHT

JEANETTE R. LYNTON

GIBBS SMITH
TO ENRICH AND INSPIRE HUMANKIND

JEANETTE R. LYNTON

Since the 1970s, Jeanette has enjoyed a passion for preserving treasured memories, and early in life began creating exclusive stamps and sharing her scrapbooking knowledge. Today, Close To My Heart, the company Jeanette founded, is a leader in the scrapbooking and stamping industry, owning many of the categories that dominate the market, including true 12" × 12" scrapbook albums, double-sided background and texture paper, lay-flat page protectors, and clear stamps.

Always at the forefront of innovation and creativity, Jeanette's pioneering products include a series of instruction programs offering simple guidelines for dynamic scrapbooking layouts and inspiring easy-to-make cards. These best-selling books continue to delight and instruct novice and expert crafters alike.

Jeanette's artistic eye and "let me show you how®" approach have made scrapbooking faster, simpler, and easier than ever before, while continuing to enhance the art of preserving memories and celebrating relationships. To learn more about Jeanette, visit her blog at jeanettelynton.com.

Dear friends,

For me, scrapbooking has always been magical. Bringing photos, paper, embellishments, and story together to preserve a treasured memory is one of the best feelings in the world—it can take my breath away more than any sleight of hand. In this book, I've taken the magic of scrapbooking one step further to interactivity. On the pages of this book, I'll guide you through tricks that surprise and delight. You'll find unique ways to hide journaling, reveal photos, and incorporate moveable elements easily to add interest, dimension, and sheer fun. I guarantee you'll savor your scrapbooks even more, returning to your magical pages again and again.

As I was developing this book, I found that each pattern had an individual personality. Some were playful and silly. Others were sweet. All opened up like an unlocked puzzle or a blossoming flower to reveal something new and different as I expanded the interactive design. In many ways, the patterns are a lot like the people in my life: happy, goofy, thoughtful, complex, or straightforward. And every friend or family member has more than just one facet. As I get to know them, they open up, showing their diversity, sharing their secrets. There's always more to learn from my dear ones, just as there's always more to explore in scrapbooking. You simply need the desire to work your own magic!

That's the fun of this book. There are so many ways to interpret each pattern to make those secrets your own. You can incorporate several interactive pieces or choose to minimize them and follow the base pattern to create a very traditional page. Each pattern offers endless creativity! And don't worry, I've provided complete instructions and detailed photography so you'll quickly and easily master all my tips and tricks.

Your life is already full of magic—now bring it to your scrapbook pages! Wishing you a life of love, days of wonder, and the endless joys of creativity,

Jeanette

Jeanette R. Lynton

{ Jeanette's TIP }

I love applying the interactive techniques to all the different patterns in this book. When you mix and match the techniques with various patterns, you create a scrapbook full of fun and surprises! One of the best ways to refresh your creativity is to approach scrapbooking playfully. Experiment with combining the techniques with patterns from my other scrapbooking books, Cherish™, Imagine™, and Reflections®. Rotate the patterns for new looks, and change up your paper and embellishments to keep each layout fresh and new.

Surprise!

Remember the feeling of going to a magic show—the delight and

awe at simple tricks that engendered glorious astonishment?

When friends look through your scrapbooks, they will feel the

same tingle of excitement. They'll discover hidden photos,

journaling buried like treasure, and secret compartments filled

with surprises… all brought to life by you, the scrapbook magician!

GETTING STARTED

Whether you're a beginner or a longtime scrapbooker, you'll find patterns and techniques in this book that are perfect for you and your magical memories. You'll find traditional, non-interactive layouts as well as interactive ones, giving you the choice to be as creative as you desire. And you'll love that many of the interactive techniques can be applied to any scrapbook pattern! Here are a few things to keep in mind as you adapt the techniques to different patterns:

• No matter which pattern you choose, moving elements and the pieces that hold them get a lot of use. Make sure you use plenty of strong adhesive and add cardstock layers to reinforce where needed.

• Where interactive pieces are folded, be sure to use a bone folder or stylus to score the piece, then work the folds back and forth to make them extra pliable.

• Memorabilia such as brochures, ticket stubs, and postcards make great additions to a layout, but can quickly clutter up a page. The techniques shown here let you turn your memorabilia into clever surprises waiting to be discovered!

• You can create a pocket for a tag or slider from any element in a pattern. Use 3-D foam tape to pop up photos, cardstock, and Background and Texture (B&T) paper.

• Even the more complex techniques can be sized up or down as needed. Be sure to carefully think through the measurements as you convert them, and remember to add stoppers to keep sliding elements from slipping out of the page!

• The enclosed DVD features technique highlights and templates for creating tags, sliders, envelopes, and more. We've added bonus templates to give you more size options!

Remember, the most important part of scrapbook magic is having fun!

Cutting Memory Protectors® for Interactive Elements

When you create interactive page elements, access them without removing the page from its Memory Protector. Let us show you how to cut your Memory Protectors® safely and effectively to minimize the chance of accidental tearing.

STEP-BY-STEP INSTRUCTIONS

1 Place completed page inside the Memory Protector. Use a stylus or bone folder to score around the area you wish to cut.

3 With the cutting mat still inside the Memory Protector, use a craft knife and ruler to cut along score line. Move the cutting mat as needed to protect the back side of the Memory Protector.

2 Remove page from Memory Protector. With a cutting mat inside the Memory Protector, punch holes at ends of score line to prevent tearing.

4 Reinsert page into Memory Protector, pulling interactive piece to outside of Memory Protector as needed.

Technique Reference

Cutting Memory Protectors®	7
STORIES IN DISGUISE	12
Memorabilia Envelopes	16
Journal Pullouts	20
Revolving Door	26
Fancy Folds	32
VANISHING ACT	38
Photo Waterfall	44
Button Slide	52
Filmstrip	58
Card Slide	64
Photo Slide	68
PRESTO CHANGE-O	72
Photo Flaps	84
Flip Flaps™	92
Explosion Flaps	100
SHOW STOPPER	104
Frame-Up	108
Accordion Booklet	118
Tag Booklet	124

PARLOR TRICK
8 photos

PAGE 14

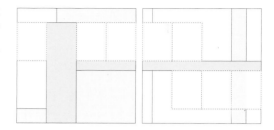

LOVE POTION
6 photos

PAGE 18

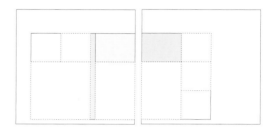

NOW YOU SEE IT
4 photos

PAGE 22

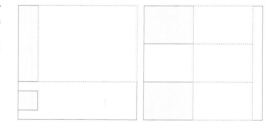

CRYSTAL BALL
5 photos

PAGE 24

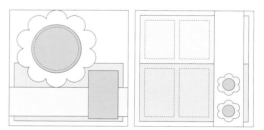

BACKSTAGE
4 photos

PAGE 28

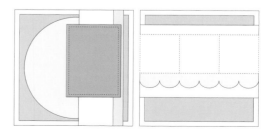

DECK OF CARDS
5 photos

PAGE 30

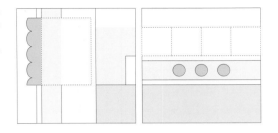

PERFORMANCE
3 photos

PAGE 48

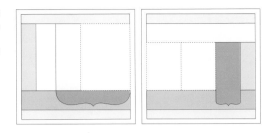

MESMERIZE
8 photos

PAGE 34

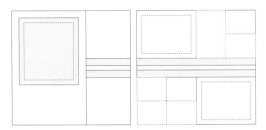

SPELLBOUND
6 photos

PAGE 50

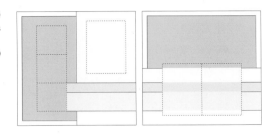

MYSTIFY
4 photos

PAGE 36

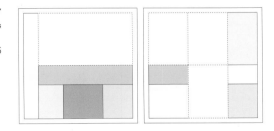

HAT TRICK
3 photos

PAGE 54

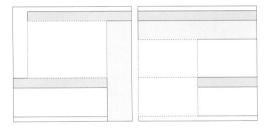

LEVITATE
4 photos

PAGE 40

HOCUS POCUS
7 photos

PAGE 56

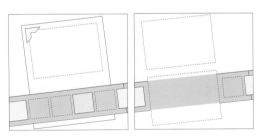

SHUFFLED DECK
7 photos

PAGE 42

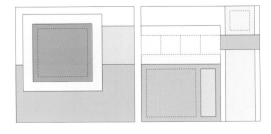

ON WITH THE SHOW
3 photos

PAGE 62

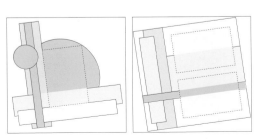

RAISE THE CURTAIN
6 photos

PAGE 66

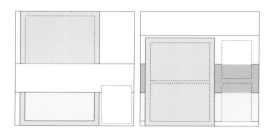

TA-DA!
4 photos

PAGE 70

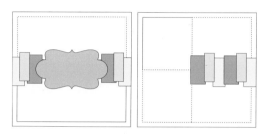

DISAPPEARING ACT
4 photos

PAGE 74

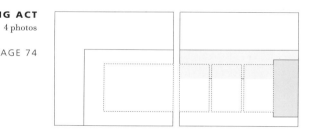

TRAP DOOR
3 photos

PAGE 76

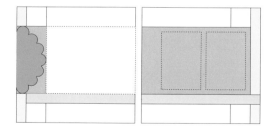

ENCHANTMENT
4 photos

PAGE 78

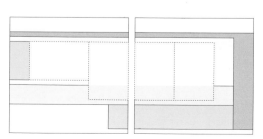

CHARMED
5 photos

PAGE 80

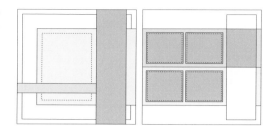

OUT OF THE HAT
9 photos

PAGE 82

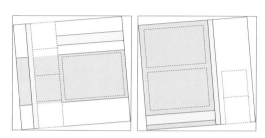

CARD TRICK
5 photos

PAGE 86

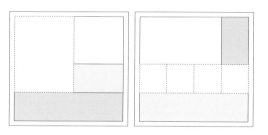

ONE-WAY MIRROR
4 photos

PAGE 88

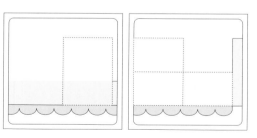

MAGIC ACT
3 photos

PAGE 90

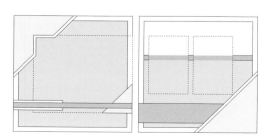

ILLUSION
4 photos

PAGE 94

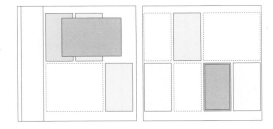

TRANSFIGURE
4 photos

PAGE 112

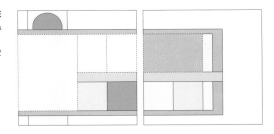

**LOVELY
ASSISTANT**
5 photos

PAGE 96

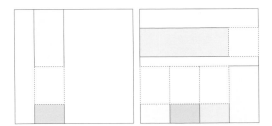

TOP HAT
5 photos

PAGE 114

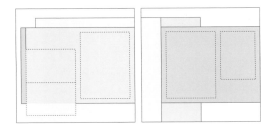

ABRACADABRA
5 photos

PAGE 98

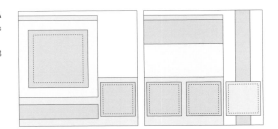

**MAGICIAN'S
CHOICE**
6 photos

PAGE 116

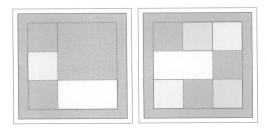

SHOWTIME
6 photos

PAGE 106

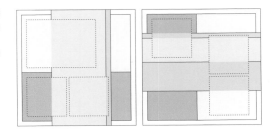

SECRET
5 photos

PAGE 120

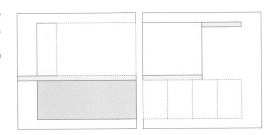

JUGGLING ACT
4 photos

PAGE 110

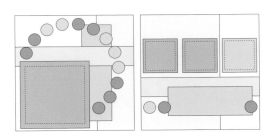

FINAL ACT
3 photos

PAGE 122

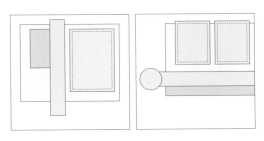

Stories in *Disguise*

They say a magician never reveals his secrets, so why should a scrapbooker? Perhaps you hide your journaling to make more room for photos, to tell another side of the story, to make your layout more interactive, or simply to keep some memories private. No matter what your reason, you'll find plenty of ways here to disguise your stories.

Beautiful 18

I hope you never lose your sense
of wonder
You get your fill to eat
But always keep that hunger
May you never take one single breath
for granted
God forbid love ever leave you
empty handed
I hope you still feel small
When you stand by the ocean
Whenever one door closes,
I hope one more opens
Promise me you'll give faith a
fighting chance

I hope you never fear those mountains
in the distance
Never settle for the path
of least resistance
Living might mean taking chances
But they're worth taking
Lovin' might be a mistake
But it's worth making
Don't let some hell bent heart
Leave you better
When you come close to selling out
Reconsider
Give the heavens above
More than just a passing glance

And when you get the chance to sit it out
or dance
I hope you dance

CUTTING INSTRUCTIONS

B&T Paper

	F 1½ × 4
H 12 × 8	**B** 5 × 3
	SCRAP

B&T Paper

G 1½ × 8	
D 5½ × 6	
A 1½ × 3	
I 12 × 1½	
	SCRAP

Cardstock

J 1 × 12	
E 1 × 6	
C 10½ × 3	
	SCRAP

Parlor Trick™

LAYOUT MATERIALS

12" × 12" Base Cardstock (2)
12" × 12" Cardstock (1)
12" × 12" B&T Paper (2)

PHOTO SUGGESTIONS

1   4" × 3" (8)

**SUGGESTED TITLE/
JOURNALING**

1   10" × 2½"

F

G

C

Photo 1
4 × 3

Photo 1
4 × 3

Photo 1
4 × 3

B

Title/Journal
10 × 2½

E

D

A

H

5½"

I

Photo 1
4 × 3

Photo 1
4 × 3

J

1"

Photo 1
4 × 3

Photo 1
4 × 3

Photo 1
4 × 3

LEFT PAGE DIMENSIONS

A   1½" × 3"
B   5" × 3"
C   10½" × 3"
D   5½" × 6"
E   1" × 6"
F   1½" × 4"
G   1½" × 8"

RIGHT PAGE DIMENSIONS

H   12" × 8"
I   12" × 1½"
J   1" × 12"

*Replace a series
of photos with an
envelope that can
hide all sorts of
surprises. Turn
the page to let the
magic begin!*

Memorabilia Envelopes

Envelopes represent endless possibilities. They can hide snapshots or lists, ticket stubs or perfume-scented love letters, and they can be attached to any page. Use the templates on the DVD to create an envelope that's just the right size to hold whatever captures your imagination!

1 Print Memorabilia Envelope template from enclosed DVD. Use template to cut envelope from cardstock or B&T paper.

2 Score envelope flaps. Embellish envelope as desired.

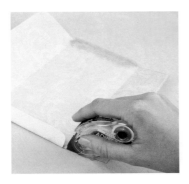

3 Fold and attach envelope flaps, leaving top flap free.

5 Attach envelope to page in place of one or more photos or pattern pieces. Place memorabilia in envelope.

4 Create closure for envelope.

6 Use hole punch and craft knife to cut opening in Memory Protector around edges of envelope.*

* See page 7 for instructions on cutting Memory Protectors®.

PROJECT VARIATION

Memorabilia Envelopes can be made using either cardstock or Background and Texture (B&T) paper. For the *Love Potion* pattern featured in this artwork, see page 18.

{ *Jeanette's* TIP }

You can replace any part of a pattern with an envelope: photo, journaling block, cardstock piece, or Background and Texture (B&T) paper piece.

PICTURE perfect

ROAD TRIP

remember this

TIMELESS
IN
Seattle

Amazing scenery, restaurants to die for, and fabulous shopping! Seattle was a total blast! we all had tons of fun switching roles as photographer and fashion model at the public market. I absolutely loved the 'artsy' metropolitan vibe there. I was so inspired just taking it all in! After visiting Pike Place—also very cool, Mindy discovered the greatest little vintage boutique. we all spent way too much money, but it was totally worth it! Seattle definitely did not disappoint us city girls!

[MeMORY]

CUTTING INSTRUCTIONS

B&T Paper

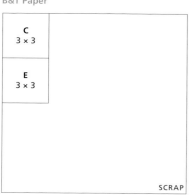

C
3 × 3

E
3 × 3

SCRAP

B&T Paper

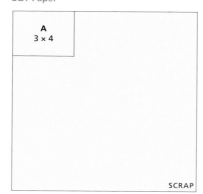

A
3 × 4

SCRAP

Cardstock

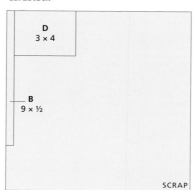

D
3 × 4

B
9 × ½

SCRAP

Love Potion™

LAYOUT MATERIALS

12" × 12" Base Cardstock (2)
12" × 12" Cardstock (1)
12" × 12" B&T Paper (2)

PHOTO SUGGESTIONS

1   6" × 6"
2   3" × 3" (3)
3   6" × 4" (2)

**SUGGESTED
JOURNALING/TITLE**

8½" × 4½"

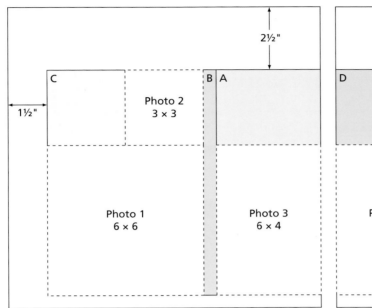

2½"

1½"

C

B A

Photo 2
3 × 3

Photo 1
6 × 6

Photo 3
6 × 4

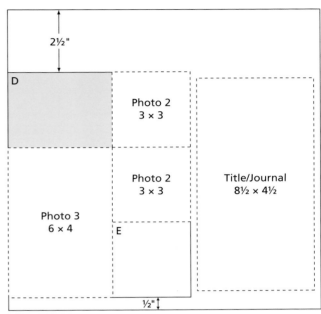

2½"

D

Photo 2
3 × 3

Photo 2
3 × 3

Title/Journal
8½ × 4½

Photo 3
6 × 4

E

½"

LEFT PAGE DIMENSIONS

A 3" × 4"
B 9" × ½"
C 3" × 3"

RIGHT PAGE DIMENSIONS

D 3" × 4"
E 3" × 3"

Extra tidbits of information can bring your story to life. Slip a few Journal Pullouts under your photos for just a bit more journaling space. Turn the page to let the magic begin!

Journal Pullouts

Add some extra journaling and a little fun to your layout with the addition of Journal Pullouts. These entertaining elements can conceal secret messages or simply hide the details of your adventures to keep the focus on the photos.

1 Cut journaling strip, allowing ½" on each end for stopper and pull tab.

2 Cut from cardstock a second journaling strip the same size as the first; attach to back of original journaling strip to reinforce. Embellish journaling strip as desired.

3 Cut two stopper pieces 1" taller than the journaling strip and ¼" wide. Layer and attach together cardstock stopper pieces. Center and attach on end of strip that will be hidden under finished page.

7 Cut from cardstock a cover 2" taller and 2" wider than journaling strip. Slip inside Memory Protector and attach to back of page, over the strip, to protect strip from catching on page behind it.

* See page 7 for instructions on cutting Memory Protectors®.

4 Determine placement of pullout, preferably where a seam exists between papers or photos. Use a craft knife to cut slit along seam where pullout will be placed. Use hole punch and craft knife to cut slit in Memory Protector for journaling pullout.*

5 Insert journaling strip from back side of page through slit in page and Memory Protector.

{ *Jeanette's* TIPS }

Since your journal pullout will be sliding in and out of the page, it's a good idea to reinforce it. By backing the pullout with cardstock, you'll help prevent accidental bends or tears.

In addition to protecting the journal pullout, the cover on the back side of the page provides a track for the pullout and stopper to slide. I try to make the cover fit snugly against where I want the stopper to slide. This helps the pullout extend in a straight line and keeps it from getting stuck.

6 Attach pull tab to journaling strip, then slide strip fully into page in closed position.

PROJECT VARIATION

Stoppers keep the pullouts from being removed from the layout and getting damaged or lost. For the *Hat Trick* pattern featured in this artwork, see page 54.

when i found out i was pregnant with tyler all of my friends kept asking me if i was disappointed to be having a boy rather than a girl. at the time i must admit i was a little bummed because having a baby girl is like having a life-sized barbie but as tyler began to grow up i found out just how much fun being the mother of boys can be. then when tyler was just four andrew came along and i wondered if i was going to survive having not one but two active little boys. luckily i have survived and now the boys are 13 & 9 and we have so much fun together. today we spent an entire afternoon up the canyon fishing and of course snapping photos for mom's scrapbook. i must say, when i look at these photos of my boys, i wouldn't change a thing.

CUTTING INSTRUCTIONS

B&T Paper

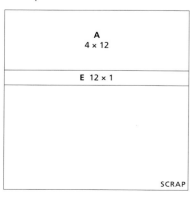

A 4 × 12	
E 12 × 1	
	SCRAP

B&T Paper

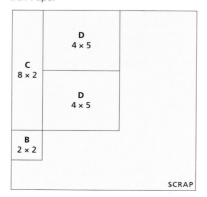

	D 4 × 5	
C 8 × 2	**D** 4 × 5	
B 2 × 2		SCRAP

Stories in
Disguise

Now You See It™

LAYOUT MATERIALS

12" × 12" Base Cardstock (2)
12" × 12" B&T Paper (2)

PHOTO SUGGESTIONS

1 8" × 10"
2 4" × 6" (3)

SUGGESTED TITLE

1 3" × 8½"

SUGGESTED JOURNALING

1 3½" × 4½"

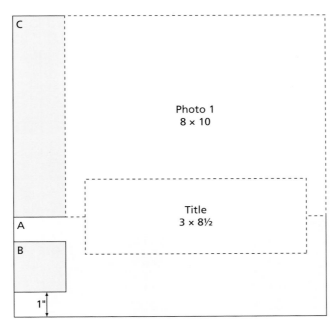

C

Photo 1
8 × 10

A

B

Title
3 × 8½

1"

D   E

Photo 2
4 × 6

Journal
3½ × 4½

Photo 2
4 × 6

D

Photo 2
4 × 6

LEFT PAGE DIMENSIONS

A 4" × 12"
B 2" × 2"
C 8" × 2"

RIGHT PAGE DIMENSIONS

D 4" × 5" (2)
E 12" × 1"

{ *Jeanette's* TIP }

A picture is worth a thousand words, so go ahead
and tell your story. Cut a window in the page
to reveal part of a pullout, placing journaling
or another photo behind the moving piece.

I know I am their mom and I may be slightly biased, but every time I look at my girls I am both surprised and amazed at how beautiful they are. ariana has such a natural beauty and grace about her. I can't believe how quickly she is growing up. serena is always so willing to help me whether it is with dinner or watching the little ones. I don't know how I would survive without her. melia is such a sweetheart and is always concerned about other people and their feelings. she is my little peacemaker. and my silly julia is the life of the party, always telling jokes and singing funny original songs that she makes up. while each of my girls are so different from one another, they are all so special to me in their own unique way.

UNIQUE

julia

serena

ariana

melia

Special

2009

CUTTING INSTRUCTIONS

B&T Paper

H
12 × 3

D
8¼ × 8¼

B&T Paper

B
3 × 12

F
5 × 11

I
2½ × 2½

I
2½ × 2½

SCRAP

Cardstock

A
6 × 11

G
6 × 11

SCRAP

Cardstock

E
5¼ × 5¼

C
5 × 3

J
1½ × 1½

SCRAP

Crystal Ball™

LAYOUT MATERIALS

12" × 12" Base Cardstock (2)
12" × 12" Cardstock (2)
12" × 12" B&T Paper (2)

PHOTO SUGGESTIONS

1 4½" Circle
2 4" × 3" (2)
3 5" × 3" (2)

SUGGESTED TITLE

1 2½" × 7"

SUGGESTED JOURNALING

1 4½" × 2½"

* See *Crystal Ball* templates
on enclosed DVD.

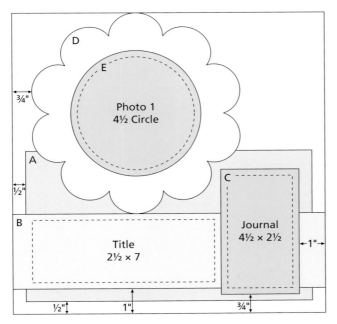

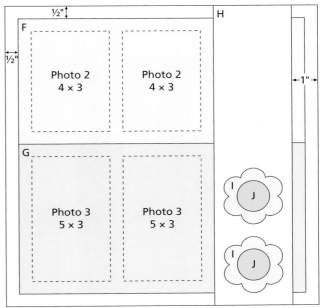

LEFT PAGE DIMENSIONS

A 6" × 11"
B 3" × 12"
C 5" × 3"
D 8¼" × 8¼" *
E 5" Circle*

RIGHT PAGE DIMENSIONS

F 5" × 11"
G 6" × 11"
H 12" × 3"
I 2½" × 2½" * (2)
J 1¼" Circle* (2)

Add a slice of life to your page with extra journaling and photos instead of one large circular photo. Turn the page to let the magic begin!

Revolving Door

You might remember these spinners from elementary school, when one opening would show a vocabulary word and the other a picture. We've updated the technique to bring a childlike playfulness to a look that's all grown up!

STEP-BY-STEP INSTRUCTIONS

1 Print Revolving Door templates from enclosed DVD. Use templates to cut technique materials. *(For the Crystal Ball pattern, we used the Revolving Door 5" templates.)*

2 Piece wedges together to form a circle.

3 Reinforce spinner by backing with cardstock.

4 Mount spinner a second time using 3-D foam tape to create dimension.

5 Insert page into Memory Protector and place cutting mat inside protector behind page to ensure back of protector is not cut. Pierce hole through page and front of protector in the center of the circle.

6 Use brad to attach stacked pieces on top of Memory Protector.

{ *Jeanette's* TIP }

If you decide to create a smaller Revolving Door, reduce the number of wedges from six to four.

PROJECT VARIATION

Create a Revolving Door in a snap! See the enclosed DVD for printable page spinner templates ranging in size from 3" to 5". For the *Levitate* pattern featured in this artwork, see page 40.

CUTTING INSTRUCTIONS

B&T Paper

G 7½ × 12
C 12 × 3½

B&T Paper

H 2 × 12

D 11 × 6

SCRAP

B&T Paper

B 12 × 1

SCRAP

Cardstock**

A 11 × 11

SCRAP

**Identical papers

Backstage™

LAYOUT MATERIALS

12" × 12" Base Cardstock (2)
12" × 12" Cardstock (3)
12" × 12" B&T Paper (3)

PHOTO SUGGESTIONS

1 7" × 5"
2 4" × 4" (3)

SUGGESTED TITLE

1 2" × 7"

SUGGESTED JOURNALING

1 3" × 3½"

* See *Backstage* templates on enclosed DVD.

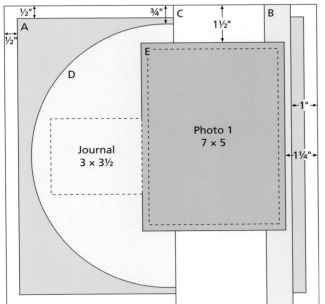

½" ¾" C   B
A   1½"
½"
E
D
Journal
3 × 3½
Photo 1
7 × 5
1"
1¼"

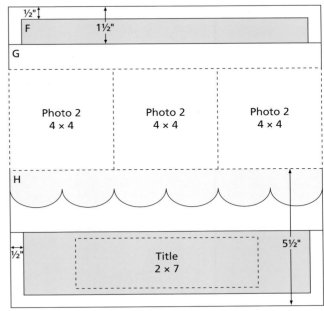

½"
F   1½"
G
Photo 2   Photo 2   Photo 2
4 × 4   4 × 4   4 × 4
H
Title
2 × 7
½"   5½"

LEFT PAGE DIMENSIONS

A 11" × 11"
B 12" × 1"
C 12" × 3½"
D 11" × 6"*
E 7½" × 5½"

RIGHT PAGE DIMENSIONS

F 11" × 11"
G 7½" × 12"
H 2" × 12"*

Cardstock**

F
11 × 11

Cardstock

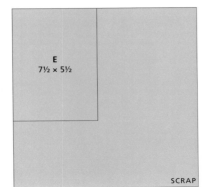

E
7½ × 5½

SCRAP

SCRAP

{ *Jeanette's* TIP }

A simple sleight of hand reveals an extra goodie hidden behind a chipboard embellishment. Use a brad to attach the chipboard piece outside the Memory Protector to both the protector and the page.

B&T Paper

		C 3 × 1
D 12 × 6	**H** 3 × 12	
		SCRAP

B&T Paper

		B 6 × 4
E 12 × 2	**I** 2 × 12	
		SCRAP

B&T Paper

G 4 × 12
A 4 × 4
SCRAP

Cardstock

F 7 × 2	**J** 1½ × 1½
	SCRAP

Deck of Cards™

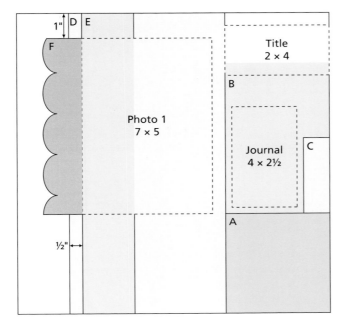

LAYOUT MATERIALS

12" × 12" Base Cardstock (2)
12" × 12" Cardstock (1)
12" × 12" B&T Paper (3)

PHOTO SUGGESTIONS

1 7" × 5"
2 3" × 3" (4)

SUGGESTED TITLE

1 2" × 4"

SUGGESTED JOURNALING

1 4" × 2½"

* See *Deck of Cards* templates
  on enclosed DVD.

Left page (diagram labels): 1", D, E, F, Photo 1 7 × 5, Title 2 × 4, B, Journal 4 × 2½, C, A, ½"

Right page (diagram labels): Photo 2 3 × 3, Photo 2 3 × 3, Photo 2 3 × 3, Photo 2 3 × 3, H, I, J ←1"→ J ←1"→ J, G

LEFT PAGE DIMENSIONS

A 4" × 4"
B 6" × 4"
C 3" × 1"
D 12" × 6"
E 12" × 2"
F 7" × 2" *

RIGHT PAGE DIMENSIONS

G 4" × 12"
H 3" × 12"
I 2" × 12"
J 1¼" Circle (3)*

*Everyone has
a story to tell,
and some are
longer than
others. When you
need more room,
create pockets
for journaling
tags. Turn the
page to let the
magic begin!*

Fancy Folds

It's time for terrific tags—with a twist! You can hide a ton of information behind a single small tag with a little creative folding. We've provided instructions for two Fancy Folds, but we're sure you'll improvise your own! For the *Deck of Cards* pattern (page 30), we used Option 1. For the *Mesmerize* pattern (page 34), we used Option 2.

{ *Jeanette's* TIP }

To really stir up memories of the event you're portraying, write about how each of your five senses was engaged in the moment. What did you see, hear, taste, smell, and touch?

FANCY FOLDS OPTION 1

1 Attach a page element on three sides using 3-D foam tape to create a pocket for the tag. Cut from cardstock a tag that is taller and narrower than the page element.

2 Cut from cardstock a strip whose height is the same as the tag height and whose length is four times the desired width of the tag plus ½". *(Example: The tag is 3¼" × 2½", so the strip is 3¼" × 10½".)*

3 Score strip vertically ½" from left side to create tab, then three more times to yield four sections the same width as the tag. Fold back and forth, accordion-style.

4 Attach ½" tab of journaling strip to tag. Place tag in pocket on page. *(Note: Cut slit in Memory Protector above pocket if desired.)*

* See page 7 for instructions on cutting Memory Protectors®.

1 Attach a page element on three sides using two layers of 3-D foam tape to create a pocket for the tag. Cut from cardstock two equally sized tags taller and narrower than the page element.

2 Measure tag. Using a lightweight paper, create journaling piece based on tag measurements.

Vertical measurement = (tag height – ½") × 3,

Horizontal measurement = (tag width – ¼") × 6.

3 Score journaling piece vertically five times and horizontally twice according to diagram 1.

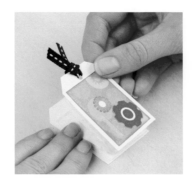

4 Fold accordion-style along vertical score marks, then fold accordion-style along horizontal score marks so that interior tag piece will fit inside tag. Attach cardstock tag pieces to top and bottom of folded interior piece. Place tag in pocket on page. (*Note: Cut slit in Memory Protector above pocket if desired.*)

* See page 7 for instructions on cutting Memory Protectors®.

DIAGRAM 1

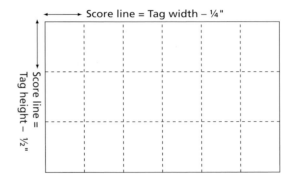

Score line = Tag width – ¼"

Score line = Tag height – ½"

{Jeanette's TIPS}

Be sure to tell the story behind your pictures! Sometimes the most important information is not the event depicted, but the relationships and interactions leading up to the moment.

Fancy Folds Option 2, folded up like a roadmap, is a great way to expand smaller tags. Turn the page to see the Mesmerize *pattern, where I've incorporated Option 2.*

CUTTING INSTRUCTIONS

© 2010 JRL PUBLICATIONS

B&T Paper

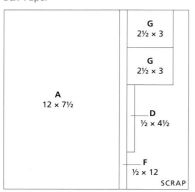

A 12 × 7½	**G** 2½ × 3
	G 2½ × 3
	D ½ × 4½
	F ½ × 12
	SCRAP

B&T Paper

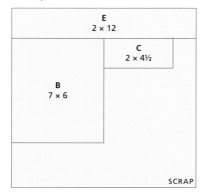

E 2 × 12	
B 7 × 6	**C** 2 × 4½
	SCRAP

34

Mesmerize™

LAYOUT MATERIALS

12" × 12" Base Cardstock (2)
12" × 12" B&T Paper (2)

PHOTO SUGGESTIONS

1 6" × 5"
2 4" × 5" (2)
3 5" × 3"
4 2½" × 3" (4)

SUGGESTED TITLE

1 2" × 6"

SUGGESTED JOURNALING

1 4" × 3"

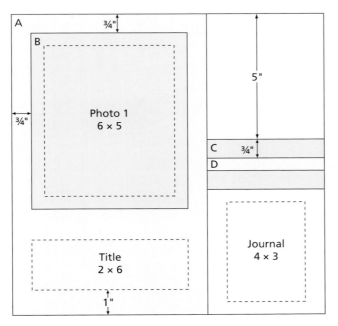

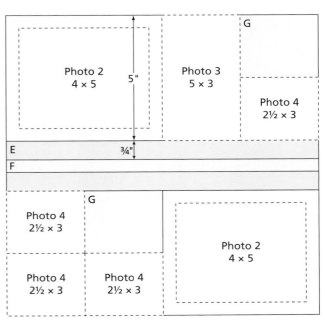

LEFT PAGE DIMENSIONS

A 12" × 7½"
B 7" × 6"
C 2" × 4½"
D ½" × 4½"

RIGHT PAGE DIMENSIONS

E 2" × 12"
F ½" × 12"
G 2½" × 3" (2)

A little fancy folding can make lots of journaling space magically appear, even in photo-filled patterns. Turn back to page 33 to let the magic begin!

family

The Zimmermans
Jen, Kal, Will, Jon, Natalie at a
nature park in Fridley,
Minnesota. A beautiful fall day
for our annual
family photo shoot
September 2009

of 5

pull

CUTTING INSTRUCTIONS

B&T Paper

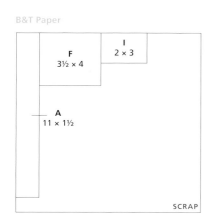

F
3½ × 4

I
2 × 3

J
5½ × 3

A
11 × 1½

SCRAP

B&T Paper

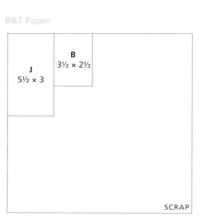

B
3½ × 2½

SCRAP

B&T Paper

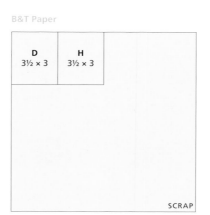

D
3½ × 3

H
3½ × 3

SCRAP

Cardstock

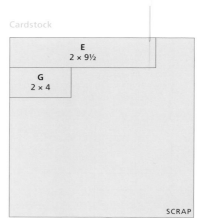

E
2 × 9½

G
2 × 4

SCRAP

Mystify™

LAYOUT MATERIALS

12" × 12" Base Cardstock (2)
12" × 12" Cardstock (2)
12" × 12" B&T Paper (3)

PHOTO SUGGESTIONS

1 5½" × 9½"
2 5½" × 4" (3)

SUGGESTED TITLE

1 1½" × 9"

SUGGESTED JOURNALING

1 3" × 3½"

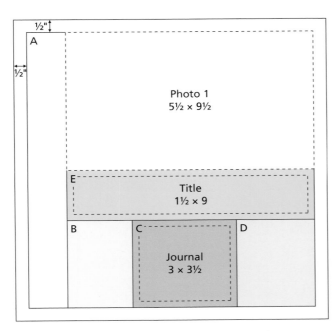

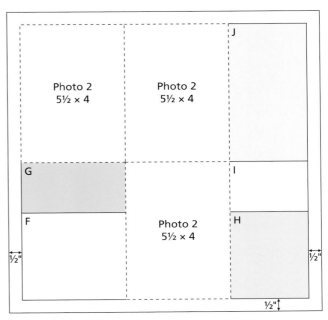

LEFT PAGE DIMENSIONS

A 11" × 1½"
B 3½" × 2½"
C 3½" × 4"
D 3½" × 3"
E 2" × 9½"

RIGHT PAGE DIMENSIONS

F 3½" × 4"
G 2" × 4"
H 3½" × 3"
I 2" × 3"
J 5½" × 3"

Cardstock

{Jeanette's TIP}

Make sure your pullouts pull toward the outsides of your album, not across the center of the album. This will help to avoid creasing or tearing them if your album is closed before the pullout is returned to its proper place.

Vanishing Act

Now you see it, now you don't! One of a magician's favorite tricks is to make something vanish into thin air . . . and then make it reappear. The techniques in this section utilize trapdoors, pulleys, and hidden compartments to hide and reveal your memorabilia. Discovering these sliding elements will make looking at your scrapbook just as exciting as the illusions in a magic show!

What a joy it is to watch you grow into such a beautiful young girl. Amazingly, your disposition is just

Homecoming DANCE

Russell and Brittney attended Homecoming Dance together at Pleasant Grove High School. They are both juniors this year and were excited to be attending their very first Homecoming. Before they left for their date we had a little photo shoot in the front yard. They were great models, goofing around and having fun together. I loved their fun attitudes, striking poses just like the pro's. It was a great evening for both of them.

Fall 2009

CUTTING INSTRUCTIONS

B&T Paper

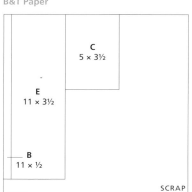

C
5 × 3½

E
11 × 3½

B
11 × ½

SCRAP

B&T Paper

F 1 × 10½

D 1 × 7

SCRAP

Cardstock

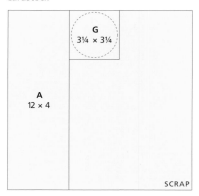

G
3¼ × 3¼

A
12 × 4

SCRAP

Levitate™

LAYOUT MATERIALS

12" × 12" Base Cardstock (2)
12" × 12" Cardstock (1)
12" × 12" B&T Paper (2)

PHOTO SUGGESTIONS

1 5" × 7" (3)
2 5" × 3½"

SUGGESTED TITLE/
JOURNALING

1 11½" × 3½"

* See *Levitate* template on
enclosed DVD.

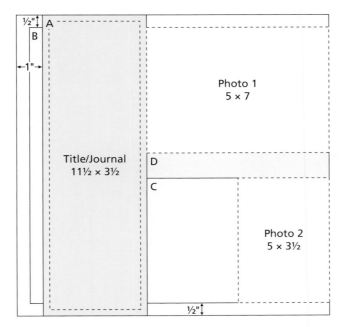

½" A
B
1"
Title/Journal
11½ × 3½
D
C
Photo 1
5 × 7
Photo 2
5 × 3½
½"

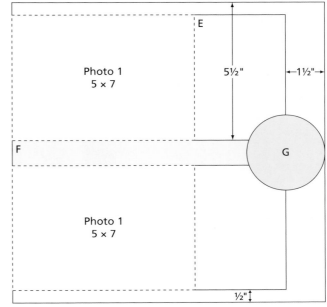

E
5½"
1½"
Photo 1
5 × 7
F
G
Photo 1
5 × 7
½"

LEFT PAGE DIMENSIONS

A 12" × 4"
B 11" × ½"
C 5" × 3½"
D 1" × 7"

RIGHT PAGE DIMENSIONS

E 11" × 3½"
F 1" × 10½"
G 3" Circle*

{ *Jeanette's* TIP }

*Give your layout an interactive
vitality by creating spinning
embellishments on the outside of the
Memory Protector. Just use a piercing
tool to make a hole in the front of the
Memory Protector so you can attach
a chipboard accent with a brad.*

CUTTING INSTRUCTIONS

B&T Paper

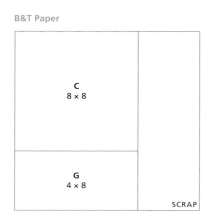

C
8 × 8

G
4 × 8

SCRAP

B&T Paper

H
12 × 3

SCRAP

B&T Paper

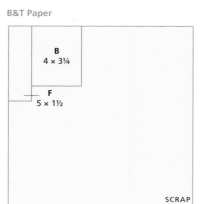

B
4 × 3¼

F
5 × 1½

SCRAP

Cardstock

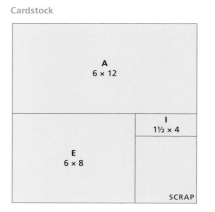

A
6 × 12

I
1½ × 4

E
6 × 8

SCRAP

Shuffled Deck™

LAYOUT MATERIALS

12" × 12" Base Cardstock (2)
12" × 12" Cardstock (2)
12" × 12" B&T Paper (3)

PHOTO SUGGESTIONS

1 5" × 5" (2)
2 2" × 2" (5)

SUGGESTED TITLE

1 2½" × 9"

SUGGESTED JOURNALING

1 2½" × 3"

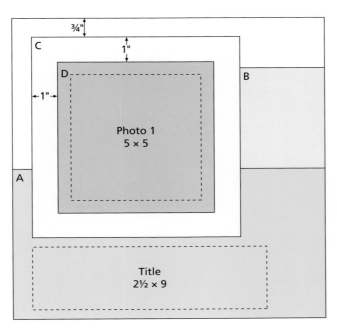

C

¾"

1"

D

1"

B

A

Photo 1
5 × 5

Title
2½ × 9

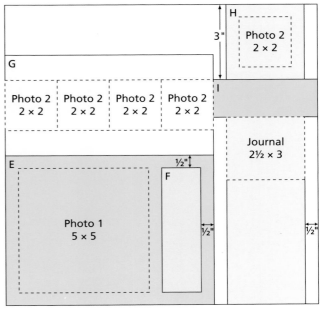

H

3"

Photo 2
2 × 2

G

I

Photo 2
2 × 2

Photo 2
2 × 2

Photo 2
2 × 2

Photo 2
2 × 2

Journal
2½ × 3

E

½"

F

Photo 1
5 × 5

½"

½"

LEFT PAGE DIMENSIONS

A 6" × 12"
B 4" × 3¼"
C 8" × 8"
D 6" × 6"

RIGHT PAGE DIMENSIONS

E 6" × 8"
F 5" × 1½"
G 4" × 8"
H 12" × 3"
I 1½" × 4"

Cardstock

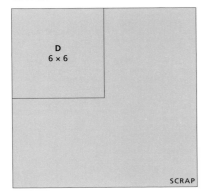

D
6 × 6

SCRAP

You can stash even more pictures in your photo lineup when you replace it with a Photo Waterfall. Turn the page to let the magic begin!

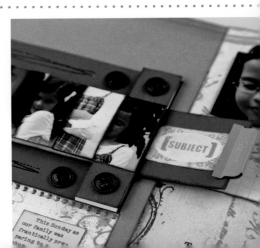

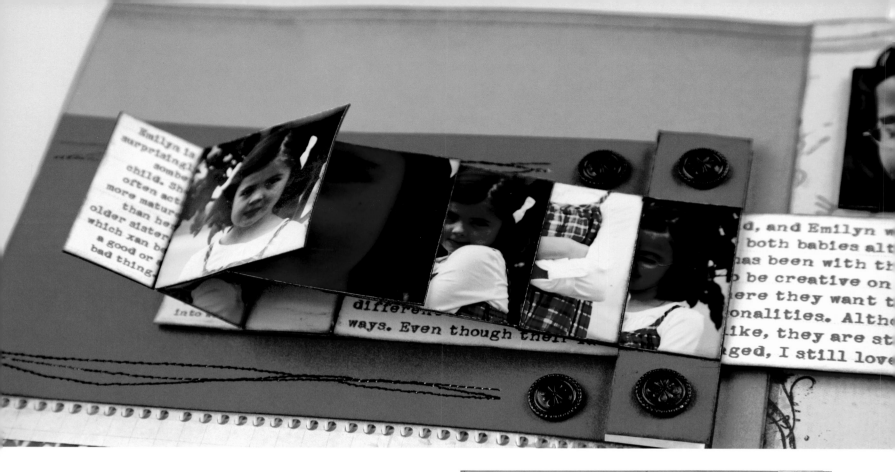

Photo Waterfall

The "wow" factor is enormous when you create a Photo Waterfall. Pull the tab and the hidden pages flip open one after another! Instead of a line of four pictures, you'll have seven 2" × 2" photos and one measuring 2" × 4", plus journaling space.

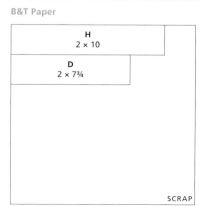

TECHNIQUE MATERIALS

A 2" × 12"
B 2" × 1" (3)
C 2" × 2" (6)
D 2" × 7¾"
E 2" × 10"
F 4" × 1" (4)
G 2" × 6"
H 2" × 10"

PHOTO SUGGESTIONS

1 2" × 4"
2 2" × 2" (7)

B&T Paper

H 2 × 10	
D 2 × 7¾	
	SCRAP

Cardstock

A 2 × 12			
E 2 × 10			C 2 × 2
G 2 × 6	C 2 × 2	C 2 × 2	C 2 × 2
F 4 × 1 / F 4 × 1 / F 4 × 1 / F 4 × 1	C 2 × 2	C 2 × 2	B 2 × 1 / B 2 × 1 / B 2 × 1
			SCRAP

DIAGRAM 1 (FRONT)

TOP

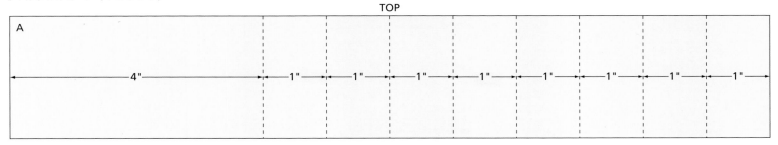

A

◄——4"——► ◄1"► ◄1"► ◄1"► ◄1"► ◄1"► ◄1"► ◄1"► ◄1"►

DIAGRAM 1 (BACK)

TOP

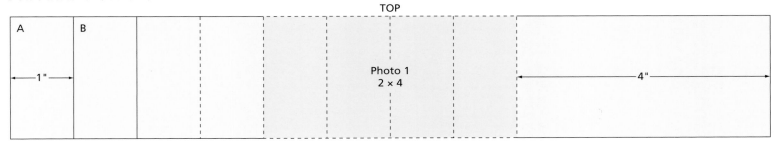

A   B

◄—1"—►

Photo 1
2 × 4

◄————4"————►

STEP-BY-STEP INSTRUCTIONS

1 Score piece A as shown in diagram 1 (front).

3 Attach six photos 2 to each piece C.

2 Score photo 1 at every inch mark. Following diagram 1 (back), attach photo 1 to piece A, lining up score marks. Layer and attach pieces B on top of each other to create a stopper. Attach pieces B to piece A.

4 Attach remaining 2" × 2" photo to front of piece A flush with right edge. Continue attaching a 1" portion of remaining mounted photos 2 to the left of first photo 2, overlapping each and keeping left edges flush with each score mark. Keep score marks clear and folds free from interference. Work folds back and forth carefully.

DIAGRAM 2 (BACK)

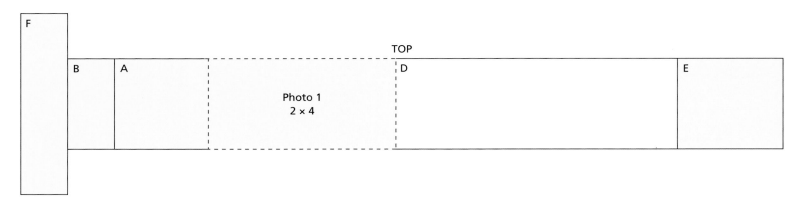

F

B A Photo 1 D TOP E
2 × 4

DIAGRAM 2 (FRONT)

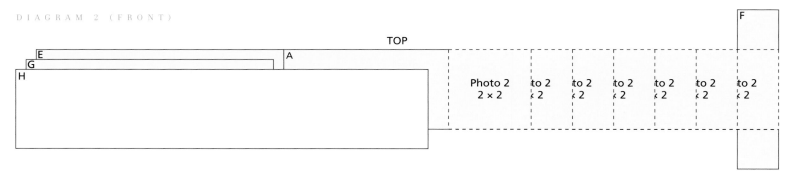

F
E A TOP
G
H Photo 2 to 2 to 2 to 2 to 2 to 2 to 2
2 × 2 ‹ 2 ‹ 2 ‹ 2 ‹ 2 ‹ 2 ‹ 2

5 Attach piece D to piece E, keeping the left edges flush.

6 Attach piece E to piece A directly to right of photo 1 as shown in diagram 2 (back).

7 Layer and attach pieces F together to create stopper. Attach pieces F to piece A as shown in diagram 2 (back).

8 Attach pieces G and H to piece E as shown in diagram 2 (front).

46

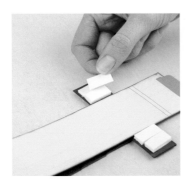

9 Fold so only portions of pieces F and piece H are exposed. Place two layers of 3-D foam tape on exposed portions of piece F.

11 Using hole punch and craft knife, cut openings in Memory Protector for pull tab and cascading photos.*

10 Keeping pieces folded, attach 3-D foam tape to page.

12 Insert page in Memory Protector, carefully bending pull tab through opening. Slowly pull tab to reveal waterfall photos.

* See page 7 for instructions on cutting Memory Protectors®.

{Jeanette's TIPS}

It can be a little tricky getting all your folds to bend smoothly when there are multiple layers. Be careful to align score marks precisely, and if the edge of a piece will be against a score mark, make sure the score mark is free from overlapping paper. Trim away any excess if necessary. Repeatedly bend folds back and forth to make them more flexible.

Moving elements can create lots of strain on the paper, so it's important that you use a strong adhesive. I recommend Liquid Glass for a durable bond. Be sure to attach all edges and corners well to prevent snagging and tearing.

When assembling your Photo Waterfall, be careful to keep all your journaling and photos right side up.

PROJECT VARIATION

A Photo Waterfall can be placed horizontally or vertically. For the *Out of the Hat* pattern featured in this artwork, turn to page 82.

B&T Paper

A 1 × 11	
A 1 × 11	
F 1 × 11	
F 1 × 11	

SCRAP

B&T Paper

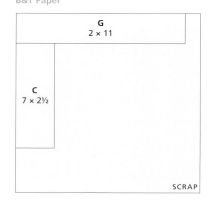

G 2 × 11

C 7 × 2½

SCRAP

B&T Paper

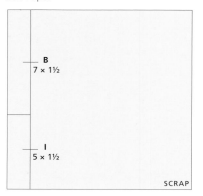

B 7 × 1½

I 5 × 1½

SCRAP

Cardstock

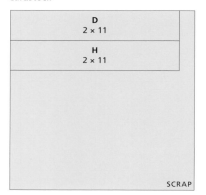

D 2 × 11

H 2 × 11

SCRAP

Performance™

LAYOUT MATERIALS

12" × 12" Base Cardstock (2)
12" × 12" Cardstock (2)
12" × 12" B&T Paper (3)

PHOTO SUGGESTIONS

1 7" × 5"
2 5" × 3½" (2)

SUGGESTED TITLE

1 ¾" × 7"

SUGGESTED JOURNALING

1 6" × 2"

* See *Performance* templates
on enclosed DVD.

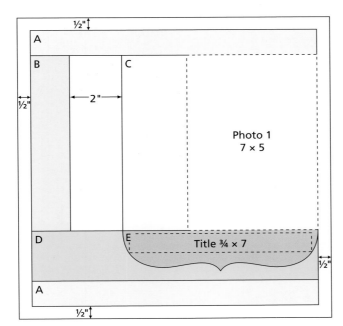

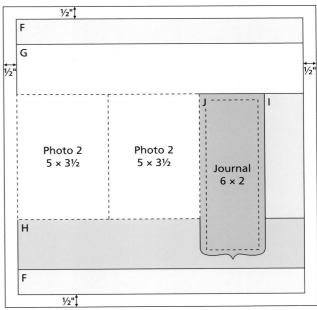

LEFT PAGE DIMENSIONS

A 1" × 11" (2)
B 7" × 1½"
C 7" × 2½"
D 2" × 11"
E 2" × 8"*

RIGHT PAGE DIMENSIONS

F 1" × 11" (2)
G 2" × 11"
H 2" × 11"
I 5" × 1½"
J 7" × 2½"*

Cardstock

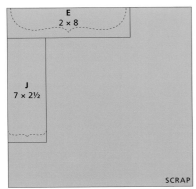

{*Jeanette's* TIP}

When creating a pocket, make sure all the pieces under it are level. Even the rise between a Background and Texture (B&T) paper and a piece of cardstock can create a ridge that can catch on the sliding piece. In this pattern, you can add a piece of paper under piece J so that the pocket is on the same level as piece G.

FEB. 21

you have
my heart, my friend,
TO HAVE AND
TO HOLD

and the DISH
ran away with the
SPOON

CUTTING INSTRUCTIONS

B&T Paper

A 12 × 6	E 6 × 12

B&T Paper

G 2 × 12

C 2 × 7

SCRAP

B&T Paper

H 1 × 12

D 1 × 7

SCRAP

Cardstock

B 11 × 5½	F 5½ × 11

SCRAP

Spellbound™

LAYOUT MATERIALS

12" × 12" Base Cardstock (2)
12" × 12" Cardstock (1)
12" × 12" B&T Paper (3)

PHOTO SUGGESTIONS

1 3" × 3" (3)
2 5½" × 4" (3)

SUGGESTED TITLE

1 2" × 6"

SUGGESTED JOURNALING

1 3" × 8"

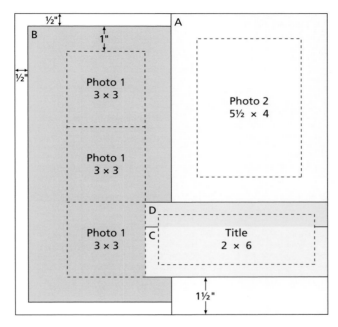

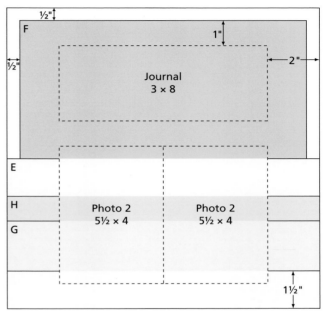

LEFT PAGE DIMENSIONS

A 12" × 6"
B 11" × 5½"
C 2" × 7"
D 1" × 7"

RIGHT PAGE DIMENSIONS

E 6" × 12"
F 5½" × 11"
G 2" × 12"
H 1" × 12"

Two photos become three when you slide open a hidden window. Turn the page to let the magic begin!

Button Slide

Use a Button Slide to showcase two versions of a similar photo or to link a pair of different photos to tell a story. What will you hide and what will you reveal?

STEP-BY-STEP INSTRUCTIONS

1 Cut around three sides of stationary photo.

2 Back sliding photo with cardstock ½" taller and ¼" wider than photo, centering top to bottom and keeping left edges flush.

3 Sew button to left edge of sliding photo.

4 On back of layout, place sliding photo next to stationary photo. Create track using 3-D foam tape extending across the length of both photos, flush with top and bottom of sliding photo.

5 Slip sliding photo, button edge first, under stationary photo.

6 Place adhesive on back of stationary photo along cut edges.

7 Cut from cardstock a cover that is twice the width and 1½" taller than the stationary photo. Attach cover to back of stationary photo and track.

8 Use hole punch and craft knife to cut ⅛" slit in Memory Protector across photo's width where button will slide.* Insert page into Memory Protector, pushing button through slit in protector.

* See page 7 for instructions on cutting Memory Protectors®.

{*Jeanette's* TIP}

For a dramatic effect, print your primary photos in sepia tones or in black and white, then let the Button Slide reveal a full-color photo.

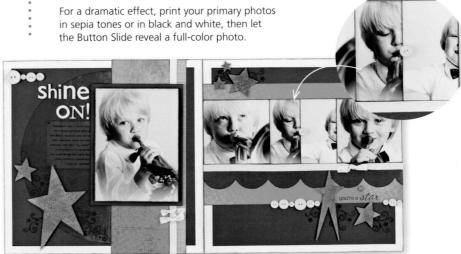

PROJECT VARIATION

To give your layout a cohesive look, use similar buttons for both the slide pull and the page accents. For the *Backstage* pattern featured in this artwork, turn to page 28.

CUTTING INSTRUCTIONS

B&T Paper

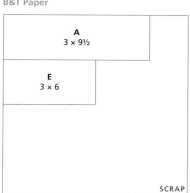

A
3 × 9½

E
3 × 6

SCRAP

B&T Paper

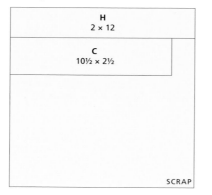

H
2 × 12

C
10½ × 2½

SCRAP

B&T Paper

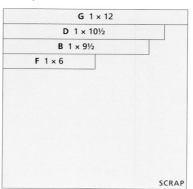

G 1 × 12
D 1 × 10½
B 1 × 9½
F 1 × 6

SCRAP

Hat Trick™

LAYOUT MATERIALS

12" × 12" Base Cardstock (2)
12" × 12" B&T Paper (3)

PHOTO SUGGESTIONS

1 6" × 8"
2 4" × 6" (2)

SUGGESTED TITLE

1 2½" × 9"

SUGGESTED JOURNALING

1 3" × 5"

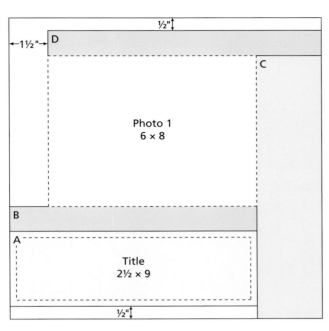

LEFT PAGE DIMENSIONS

A 3" × 9½"
B 1" × 9½"
C 10½" × 2½"
D 1" × 10½"

RIGHT PAGE DIMENSIONS

E 3" × 6"
F 1" × 6"
G 1" × 12"
H 2" × 12"

{ *Jeanette's* TIP }

When creating pull tabs, use a variety of items such as looped thread, buttons, small metal accents, stickers, or ribbon. By doing so, you keep your creativity and artwork fresh.

B&T Paper**

A
10¾ × 8¼

SCRAP

B&T Paper**

G
7½ × 12

SCRAP

B&T Paper

D
2 × 2

D
2 × 2

J
2 × 2

J
2 × 2

F
1½ × 1½

SCRAP

B&T Paper

E
2 × 2

SCRAP

**Identical papers

Hocus Pocus™

LAYOUT MATERIALS

12" × 12" Base Cardstock (2)
12" × 12" Cardstock (1)
12" × 12" B&T Paper (4)

PHOTO SUGGESTIONS

1 2" × 2" (4)
2 5" × 7" (3)

SUGGESTED TITLE

1 1½" × 6"

SUGGESTED JOURNALING

1 ⅜" × 2¼" (5)

* See *Hocus Pocus* template
   on enclosed DVD.

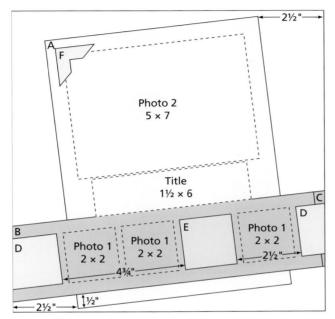

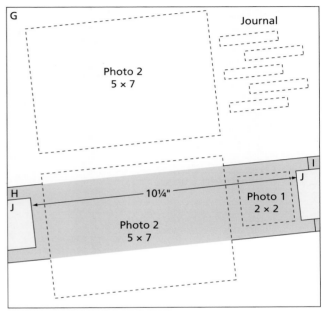

LEFT PAGE DIMENSIONS

A 10¾" × 8¼"
B 3" × 12" (trim)
C 3" × 1" (trim)
D 2" × 2" (2, trim)
E 2" × 2"
F 1½" × 1½" *

RIGHT PAGE DIMENSIONS

G 7½" × 12"
H 3" × 12" (trim)
I 3" × 1" (trim)
J 2" × 2" (2, trim)

Cardstock

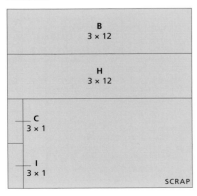

*Turn a simple
Filmstrip into a
motion picture
by adding sliding
photos. Turn the
page to let the
magic begin!*

Filmstrip

As any great film director knows, an adventure story should depict plenty of action. With the Filmstrip technique, you can transform your photos from simple stills into exciting escapades. Each photo will become a superstar!

TECHNIQUE MATERIALS

A 2¼" × 1" (3)
B 2¼" × ¾" (3)
C 2¼" × 12"
D 2¼" × 10¼" (cut from Memory Protector)
E 3" × 12"
F 3" × 1½"
G 2" × 2" (2, trim)
H 2" × 2"
I 3" × 12" (cut from Memory Protector)
J 2½" × 12"
K 2½" × ¾" (3)

PHOTO SUGGESTIONS

1 2¼" × 2¼" (5)

DIAGRAM 1

B	C			A
			Photo 1 2¼ × 2¼	

1 Layer and attach pieces A together to create a stopper. Layer and attach pieces B together to create a stopper. Attach pieces A and B and one photo 1 to piece C as shown in diagram 1.

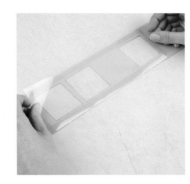

4 Attach piece I centered to back of 3" × 13" strip.

2 Attach piece C to page. *(Note: If placing piece C on a diagonal, edges may need to be trimmed flush with page.)* Attach piece D to piece C, centered between stoppers.

5 Attach ¼" 3-D foam tape to back of 3" × 13" strip along the top and bottom edges.

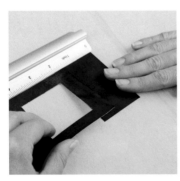

3 Attach piece E to piece E overlapping ½" to create a 3" × 13" strip. Attach pieces G, H and cut openings as shown in diagram 2.

6 Attach 3" × 13" strip to page centered over piece C. Trim right and left edges flush with base page.

DIAGRAM 2

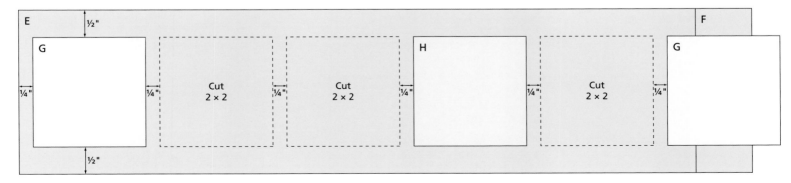

DIAGRAM 3 (FRONT)

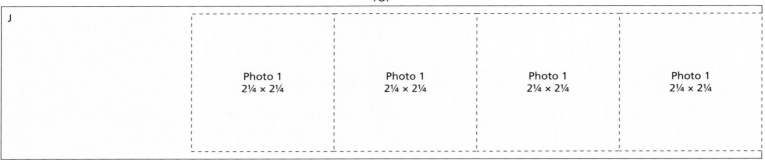

TOP

J

| Photo 1 2¼ × 2¼ | Photo 1 2¼ × 2¼ | Photo 1 2¼ × 2¼ | Photo 1 2¼ × 2¼ |

DIAGRAM 3 (BACK)

TOP

J

K

4"

7 Attach remaining photos 1 to piece J as shown in diagram 3 (front).

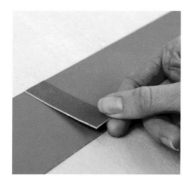

8 Layer and attach pieces K together to create a stopper. Attach pieces K to piece J as shown in diagram 3 (back).

9 Insert page into Memory Protector. Score 3" slit along outside edge of protector paralleling piece E. Remove page and use hole punch and craft knife to cut slit.*

10 Reinsert page into Memory Protector. Insert piece J into Filmstrip pocket by gently lifting stoppers over each other.

* See page 7 for instructions on cutting Memory Protectors®.

{ *Jeanette's* TIPS }

Since the Hocus Pocus pattern has a row of photos that extends through both pages, I created a Filmstrip for both the left and right pages of the layout you see above.

You may wish to embellish the pull tab at the end of your Filmstrip slider. It's best to do so after the page has already been inserted into the Memory Protector.

PROJECT VARIATION

You can create a Filmstrip anytime you have a row of same-sized photos. Use the photo placements on the pattern as a guide to size your Filmstrip. For the *Parlor Trick* pattern featured in this artwork, turn to page 14.

B&T Paper

G
10½ × 10½

D
10 × 1½

B&T Paper

C
2 × 11

H
4 × 7½

J
9½ × 1½

SCRAP

B&T Paper

A
11 × 2

I
10½ × 2

SCRAP

Cardstock

K ¾ × 10½

F
3 × 3

B
6 × 6

E
11 × ¾

SCRAP

On with the Show™

LAYOUT MATERIALS

12" × 12" Base Cardstock (2)
12" × 12" Cardstock (1)
12" × 12" B&T Paper (3)

PHOTO SUGGESTIONS

1 6" × 4"
2 4" × 6" (2)

SUGGESTED TITLE

1 1½" × 5½"

SUGGESTED JOURNALING

1 2" × 4"*

* See *On with the Show*
templates on enclosed DVD.

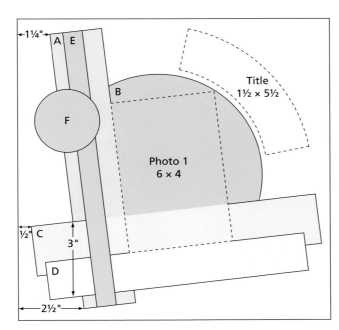

LEFT PAGE DIMENSIONS

A 11" × 2"
B 6" × 6"*
C 2" × 11"
D 10" × 1½"
E 11" × ¾"
F 2½" Circle*

RIGHT PAGE DIMENSIONS

G 10½" × 10½"
H 4" × 7½"
I 10½" × 2"
J 9½" × 1½"
K ¾" × 10½"

*Bring even more
attention to
the focal photo
by concealing
bonus elements
underneath. A
hidden pulley
makes for twice
the fun. Turn the
page to let the
magic begin!*

Card Slide

You get double the fun when you create a Card Slide as part of your page. This technique utilizes a hidden pulley so that when the tab is pulled, journaling comes out on one side and a photo pops out on the other. It's a two-for-one special!

6" × 4" CARD SLIDE

TECHNIQUE MATERIALS

A 6" × 4" (6" × 4" Card Slide Template A)
B 1½" × 7" (cut from plastic)
C 1¼" × 7" (cut from plastic)
D 4" × 3" (2)
E 1½" × 4½"
F 1½" × 3½"
G 2½" × 3"

PHOTO SUGGESTIONS

1 2½" × 3" (2½" × 2½" viewable)
2 6" × 4"

SUGGESTED JOURNALING

1 4" × 2½"

DIAGRAM 1

A

B
C — Tape
— Tape

DIAGRAM 2

D
1¼"
E
1"
Journal
4 × 2½

DIAGRAM 3

G   ½"
F

1 Trim piece A using Card Slide template from enclosed DVD. *(Note: For the* On with the Show *pattern, we used the Card Slide 6" × 4" template.)* Following diagram 1, wrap piece B around piece A and tape seam to piece A. Wrap piece C around piece B and tape seam only of piece C.

2 Following diagram 2, sandwich piece E between pieces D and add suggested journaling.

3 Following diagram 3, sandwich piece F between piece G and back of photo 1.

4 Positioning tape as shown in diagram 1, attach right tab only of piece E to piece C so that piece E is behind piece A and right side of piece E is flush with the right notch in piece A. *(Note: Journaling should face piece A.)*

5 Attach left tab only of piece F to piece C so that piece F is in front of piece A and flush with the left notch in piece A. *(Note: Photo should face upward.)*

6 Attach photo 2 to piece A using 3-D foam tape along the top and bottom only. Attach piece A to page using 3-D foam tape along the top and bottom only.

7 Insert page into Memory Protector. Score slit to left of photo 2 to accommodate pull tab and journaling. Remove page and use hole punch and craft knife to cut Memory Protector along scored lines.* Insert page in Memory Protector, bending pull tab through opening in Memory Protector.

* See page 7 for instructions on cutting Memory Protectors®.

{ Jeanette's TIPS }

The secret to getting a smooth slide is using flexible plastic for the pulley. Transparencies and Memory Protectors aren't quite pliable enough, so I recommend cutting pieces B and C from a quart-size freezer bag, avoiding the bag seams.

Try experimenting with Card Slides in various sizes. See the Card Slide templates on enclosed DVD to adapt this technique for use with photos ranging in size from 4" × 3" to 7" × 5".

bella italia

The Villa D'Este, found in Tivoli, Italy, was renovated in the 16th century to include these breath-taking fountains and gardens that delight the senses.

VILLA D'ESTE

B&T Paper

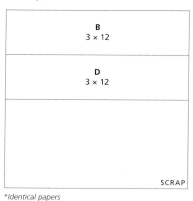

B 3 × 12	
D 3 × 12	
	SCRAP

B&T Paper

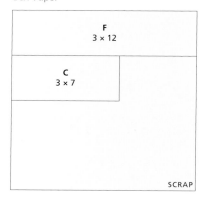

F 3 × 12	
C 3 × 7	
	SCRAP

Cardstock*

A 12 × 8	
	SCRAP

Cardstock*

G 9¼ × 7	
	SCRAP

*Identical papers

Raise the Curtain™

LAYOUT MATERIALS

12" × 12" Base Cardstock (2)
12" × 12" Cardstock (3)
12" × 12" B&T Paper (2)

PHOTO SUGGESTIONS

1 5" × 7"
2 4" × 3" (3)
3 4" × 6" (2)

SUGGESTED TITLE

1 2" × 11"

SUGGESTED JOURNALING

1 3" × 3"

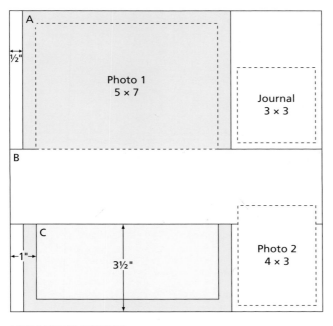

A
½"
Photo 1
5 × 7
Journal
3 × 3

B

C
1"
3½"
Photo 2
4 × 3

LEFT PAGE DIMENSIONS

A 12" × 8"
B 3" × 12"
C 3" × 7"

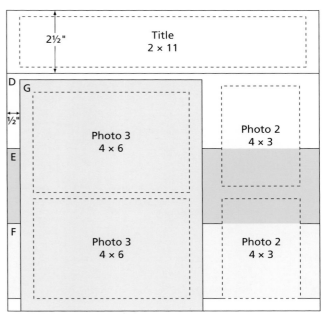

2½"   Title
2 × 11

D
G
½"
Photo 3
4 × 6
Photo 2
4 × 3

E

F
Photo 3
4 × 6
Photo 2
4 × 3

RIGHT PAGE DIMENSIONS

D 3" × 12"
E 3" × 12"
F 3" × 12"
G 9¼" × 7"

Cardstock

E
3 × 12

SCRAP

A little tug, and pop! goes the photo. Turn the page to let the magic begin!

Photo Slide

Though the technique is simple, Photo Slides pack a powerful punch. Pull the tab and the photo pops up away from the page, revealing the hidden secrets below. Add a few to your layout and you will be praised for your ingenuity!

4" × 3" PHOTO SLIDE

TECHNIQUE MATERIALS

A 4½" × 3½" (4" × 3" Photo Slide Template A)
B 5½" × 3½"

PHOTO SUGGESTION

1 4" × 3"

STEP-BY-STEP INSTRUCTIONS

1 Trim and score piece A using Photo Slide template from enclosed DVD. Work folds back and forth. *(Note: For the Raise the Curtain pattern, we used the 4" × 3" Photo Slide template.)*

68

2 Attach piece B to bottom scored flap of piece A. Piece B will extend past top, left, and right sides of flap. To allow slide to move freely, avoid adhering to frame around flap. Turn over so that piece B is underneath piece A.

3 Trim ¼" from bottom of photo. Attach ¼" photo piece to bottom scored flap on piece A, centered right to left. Ensure fold can bend easily and photo piece can move freely above frame around flap.

4 Attach bottom half only of larger photo piece to middle scored section of piece A, directly above ¼" section. Ensure photo piece can move freely.

5 Attach piece A to base page using ⅛" wide 3-D foam tape on left, bottom, and right sides only.

6 Use hole punch and craft knife to cut opening in Memory Protector around edges of mat.

7 Insert page in Memory Protector, bending top end of slide through opening to create a pull tab.

* See page 7 for instructions on cutting Memory Protectors®.

{Jeanette's TIPS}

When adhering the pull tab (piece B) and photo to the Photo Slide (piece A), ensure pieces slide freely by applying adhesive to flap rather than to the pull tab or photo.

I always use a strong adhesive such as Liquid Glass to make sure my mobile pieces are durable.

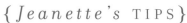

PROJECT VARIATION

Allow your Photo Slide to reveal either photos or journaling. See the Photo Slide templates on enclosed DVD to adapt this technique for use with photos ranging in size from 3" × 3" to 7" × 5". For the *Magician's Choice* pattern featured in this artwork, turn to page 116.

B&T Paper

A
6½ × 11

F
5½ × 5

SCRAP

B&T Paper

G
3 × 1¼

G
3 × 1¼

B
3 × 1¼

B
3 × 1¼

SCRAP

B&T Paper

I
3 × 1

I
3 × 1

D
3 × 1

D
3 × 1

SCRAP

Cardstock

E
4½ × 7½

SCRAP

Ta-Da!™

LAYOUT MATERIALS

12" × 12" Base Cardstock (2)
12" × 12" Cardstock (2)
12" × 12" B&T Paper (3)

PHOTO SUGGESTIONS

1 4½" × 11"
2 5½" × 5"
3 4½" × 6" (2)

SUGGESTED TITLE

1 2" × 5"

* See *Ta-Da!* template on enclosed DVD.

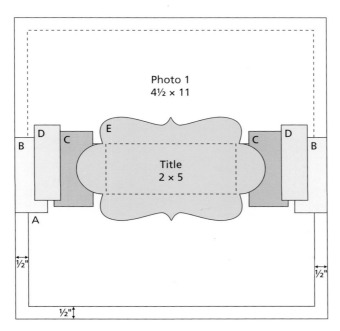

Photo 1
4½ × 11

Title
2 × 5

D C E C D
B B
A

½"
½"
½"

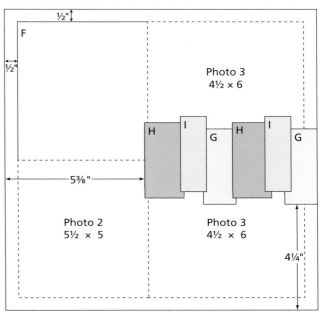

½"
½"

F

Photo 3
4½ × 6

H I G H I G

5⅜"

Photo 2
5½ × 5

Photo 3
4½ × 6

4¼"

LEFT PAGE DIMENSIONS

A 6½" × 11"
B 3" × 1¼" (2)
C 3" × 1½" (2)
D 3" × 1" (2)
E 4½" × 7½" *

RIGHT PAGE DIMENSIONS

F 5½" × 5"
G 3" × 1¼" (2)
H 3" × 1½" (2)
I 3" × 1" (2)

Cardstock

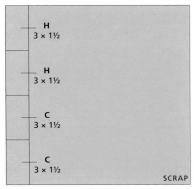

H
3 × 1½

H
3 × 1½

C
3 × 1½

C
3 × 1½

SCRAP

. . . .

{ *Jeanette's* TIP }

Putting adhesive around three sides of any rectangle will form a pocket, but adhering the pocket with 3-D foam tape gives dimension to the layout and draws attention to the interactive element.

Presto Change-O

Magicians love to amaze the audience by performing astounding transformations. A rabbit is placed in a hat and a dove emerges. A beautiful assistant enters a cage, and with a flash of smoke, a tiger appears in her place. In Presto Change-O, we'll show you how to transform a title into a journaling spot, ribbon into hinges, and a Memory Protector into a photo sleeve. We'll even demonstrate how you can turn a single page into five in a few easy steps. Read on to find these magic tricks revealed!

It's a **Beautiful** *Day!*

Getting up so early to hike Mt. Timp was not fun or easy to do. You practically have to start in the middle of the night! But it is all worth it when you get to the top in time to watch the sunrise. It was cold to begin with but warmed up a lot by mid-morning. How there can be a glacier on top of the mountain even in the middle of the summer I will never know.

american fork, ut

B&T Paper*

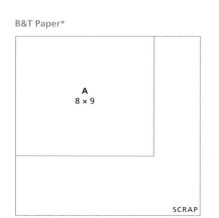

A
8 × 9

SCRAP

B&T Paper*

B
5 × 12

SCRAP

B&T Paper

C
3 × 12

SCRAP

Cardstock

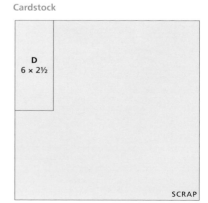

D
6 × 2½

SCRAP

*Identical papers

Disappearing Act™

LAYOUT MATERIALS

12" × 12" Base Cardstock (2)
12" × 12" Cardstock (1)
12" × 12" B&T Paper (3)

PHOTO SUGGESTIONS

1 5" × 7"
2 5" × 3" (3)

SUGGESTED TITLE

1 11" × 2½"

SUGGESTED JOURNALING

1 5½" × 2"

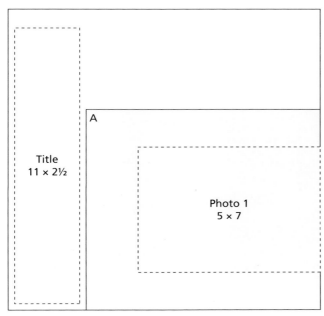

A

Title
11 × 2½

Photo 1
5 × 7

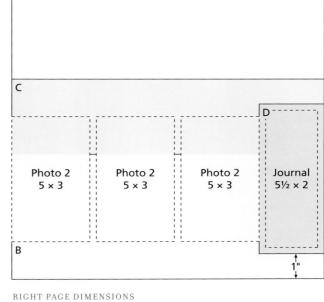

C

D

Photo 2
5 × 3

Photo 2
5 × 3

Photo 2
5 × 3

Journal
5½ × 2

B

1"

LEFT PAGE DIMENSIONS

A 8" × 9"

RIGHT PAGE DIMENSIONS

B 5" × 12"
C 3" × 12"
D 6" × 2½"

*Attach hinges
to chipboard
elements such as
this title, then
flip them open
for small or
large surprises.*

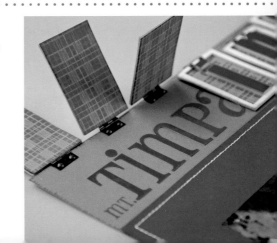

B&T Paper

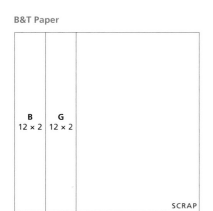

B
12 × 2

G
12 × 2

SCRAP

B&T Paper

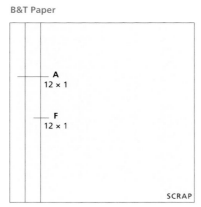

A
12 × 1

F
12 × 1

SCRAP

B&T Paper

I 1 × 12

D 1 × 11

SCRAP

Cardstock

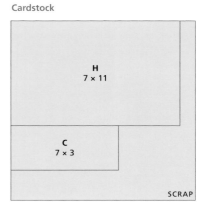

H
7 × 11

C
7 × 3

SCRAP

Trap Door™

LAYOUT MATERIALS

12" × 12" Base Cardstock (2)
12" × 12" Cardstock (2)
12" × 12" B&T Paper (3)

PHOTO SUGGESTIONS

1 7" × 9"
2 6" × 4" (2)

SUGGESTED TITLE

1 4½" × 1½"

SUGGESTED JOURNALING

1 5½" × 1½"

* See *Trap Door* template on enclosed DVD.

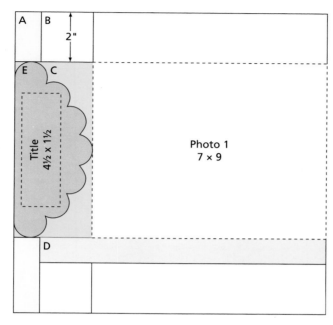

A | B
2"
E | C
Title 4½ × 1½
Photo 1 7 × 9
D

H
Journal 5½ × 1½
Photo 2 6 × 4
Photo 2 6 × 4
I

G | F
2"

LEFT PAGE DIMENSIONS

A 12" × 1"
B 12" × 2"
C 7" × 3"
D 1" × 11"
E 7½" × 3½"*

RIGHT PAGE DIMENSIONS

F 12" × 1"
G 12" × 2"
H 7" × 11"
I 1" × 12"

Cardstock

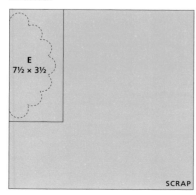

E
7½ × 3½

SCRAP

Use the title as a creative way to house journaling by putting the entire title piece on hinges and adhering your story underneath. Remember to slit the Memory Protector along the outside edge to accommodate the interactive element.

BEAUTY

"It's BEAUTY that Captures my attention: PERsoNaLITY whiCh Captures my heart."

inside & out

CUTTING INSTRUCTIONS

B&T Paper

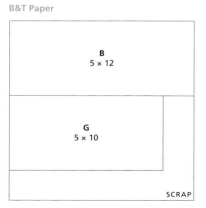

B
5 × 12

G
5 × 10

SCRAP

B&T Paper

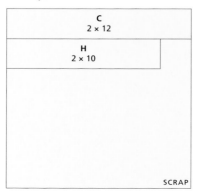

C
2 × 12

H
2 × 10

SCRAP

B&T Paper

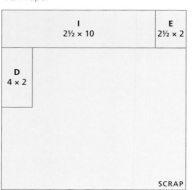

I
2½ × 10

E
2½ × 2

D
4 × 2

SCRAP

Cardstock

F
10 × 12

A ½ × 12

SCRAP

Enchantment™

LAYOUT MATERIALS

12" × 12" Base Cardstock (2)
12" × 12" Cardstock (1)
12" × 12" B&T Paper (3)

PHOTO SUGGESTIONS

1 4" × 6"
2 6" × 4" (3)

SUGGESTED TITLE

1 2½" × 6"

SUGGESTED JOURNALING

1 2½" × 10"

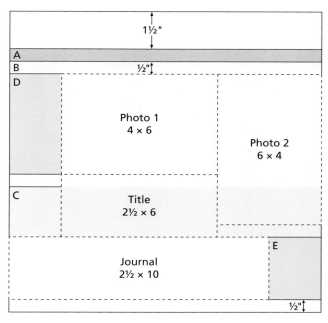

1½"

A
B   ½"
D

Photo 1
4 × 6

Photo 2
6 × 4

C   Title
2½ × 6

E

Journal
2½ × 10

½"

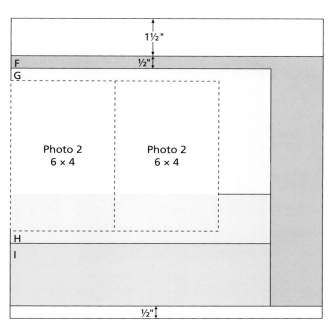

1½"

F   ½"
G

Photo 2
6 × 4

Photo 2
6 × 4

H
I

½"

LEFT PAGE DIMENSIONS

A ½" × 12"
B 5" × 12"
C 2" × 12"
D 4" × 2"
E 2½" × 2"

RIGHT PAGE DIMENSIONS

F 10" × 12"
G 5" × 10"
H 2" × 10"
I 2½" × 10"

{ *Jeanette's* TIP }

*File your memories neatly away
using the File Flap templates on the
enclosed DVD.*

SUNSHINE

Nothing but blue skies &

It's hard to believe that Dennis is already 10 years old! This year for his birthday, we surprised Big-D with a weekend trip to the ever-busy Hampton Beach in New Hampshire, a few hours from our home.

It is one of his favorite vacationing spots because there is always something new and exciting happening there. We spent almost every hour in the water!

CUTTING INSTRUCTIONS

B&T Paper*

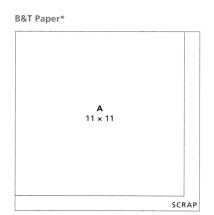

A
11 × 11

SCRAP

B&T Paper*

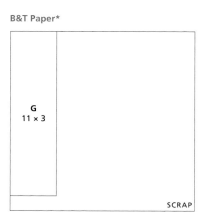

G
11 × 3

SCRAP

B&T Paper

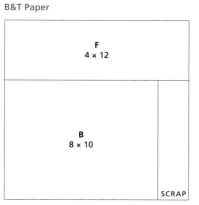

F
4 × 12

B
8 × 10

SCRAP

B&T Paper

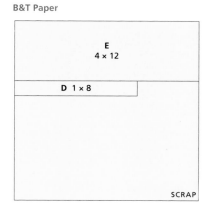

E
4 × 12

D 1 × 8

SCRAP

*Identical papers

Charmed™

LAYOUT MATERIALS

12" × 12" Base Cardstock (2)
12" × 12" Cardstock (1)
12" × 12" B&T Paper (4)

PHOTO SUGGESTIONS

1 7" × 5"
2 3" × 3½" (4)

SUGGESTED TITLE

1 10" × 2"

SUGGESTED JOURNALING

1 3½" × 2½"

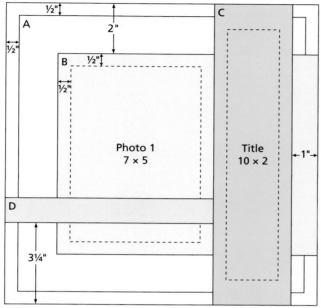

A

½"
2"
½"

B
½"
½"

Photo 1
7 × 5

C

Title
10 × 2

D
3¼"

1"

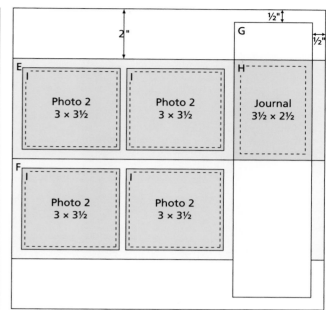

½"
2"
½"

G
½"

E
I
Photo 2
3 × 3½

I
Photo 2
3 × 3½

H
Journal
3½ × 2½

F
I
Photo 2
3 × 3½

I
Photo 2
3 × 3½

LEFT PAGE DIMENSIONS

A 11" × 11"
B 8" × 10"
C 12" × 3"
D 1" × 8"

RIGHT PAGE DIMENSIONS

E 4" × 12"
F 4" × 12"
G 11" × 3"
H 4" × 3"
I 3¼" × 3¾" (4)

Cardstock

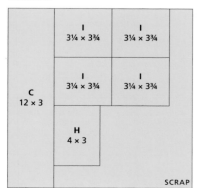

I
3¼ × 3¾

I
3¼ × 3¾

I
3¼ × 3¾

I
3¼ × 3¾

C
12 × 3

H
4 × 3

SCRAP

{*Jeanette's* TIP}

Batten down the hatches! Use a variety of embellishment combinations to keep flaps safely closed.

CUTTING INSTRUCTIONS

B&T Paper*

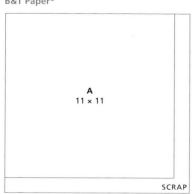

A
11 × 11

SCRAP

B&T Paper*

E
11 × 11

SCRAP

B&T Paper

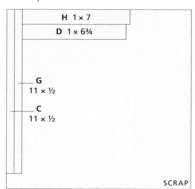

H 1 × 7

D 1 × 6¾

G
11 × ½

C
11 × ½

SCRAP

Cardstock

B
5 × 11

F
11 × 7

SCRAP

*Identical papers

Out of the Hat™

LAYOUT MATERIALS

12" × 12" Base Cardstock (2)
12" × 12" Cardstock (1)
12" × 12" B&T Paper (3)

PHOTO SUGGESTIONS

1   4½" × 6"
2   4" × 6" (2)
3   2¾" × 2½" (6)

SUGGESTED TITLE

1   2" × 6"

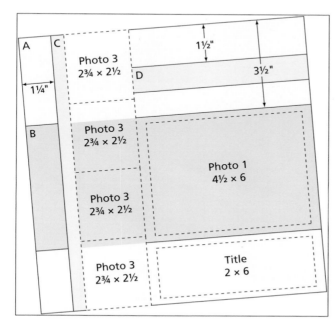

Left page (as labeled in diagram):
A | C
Photo 3
2¾ × 2½
D   1½"   3½"
1¼"
B
Photo 3
2¾ × 2½
Photo 1
4½ × 6
Photo 3
2¾ × 2½
Photo 3
2¾ × 2½
Title
2 × 6

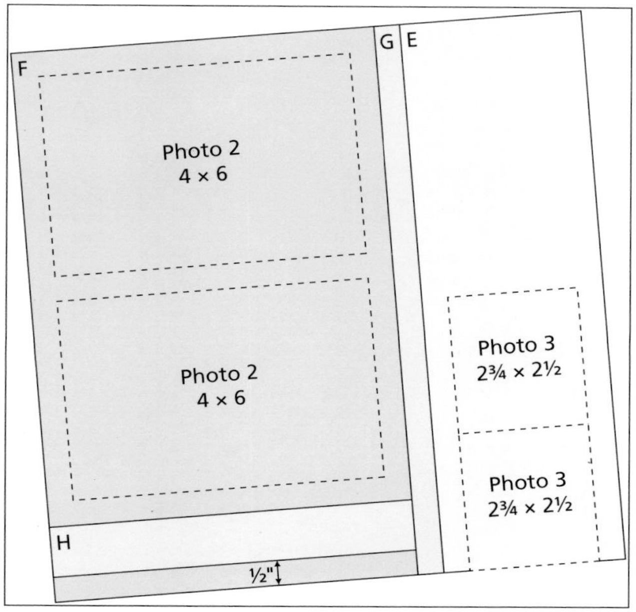

Right page (as labeled in diagram):
G E
F
Photo 2
4 × 6
Photo 2
4 × 6
Photo 3
2¾ × 2½
Photo 3
2¾ × 2½
H
½"

LEFT PAGE DIMENSIONS

A   11" × 11"
B   5" × 11"
C   11" × ½"
D   1" × 6¾"

RIGHT PAGE DIMENSIONS

E   11" × 11"
F   11" × 7"
G   11" × ½"
H   1" × 7"

The space housing one photo can actually hold seven when you stack them with Photo Flaps. Turn the page to let the magic begin!

Photo Flaps

The extra photos in this layout sit on top of the Memory Protector, but are still safe and sound inside photo sleeves. The secret ingredients are hinges and two halves of a photo storage page. Shh, don't tell!

1 Cut a 12" × 12" six-pocket photo storage page in half top to bottom. Remove binding edge of the storage page by cutting close to the seam.

2 Score along seams between photo pockets. Fold back and forth, accordion-style.

3 Fill both sides of each pocket with photos and journaling.

7 With cutting mat inside Memory Protector and behind page, use hole punch and craft knife to cut slits through Memory Protector and page to accommodate ribbon closure.

4 Use brads to attach hinges along bottom or top edge of flap, 1" from right and left sides of photo pocket. Be sure to place hinges along the edge that will be attached to the page so the flaps will fold out as desired.

8 Thread ribbon closure through slits and fasten as desired.

* See page 7 for instructions on cutting Memory Protectors®.

5 Attach ¼" × 6" strip of paper to cover brad prongs.

{Jeanette's TIP}

Just as with the pullouts described on pages 20–21 and 37, I'm always careful to position my hinges so that the flaps will extend toward the outside of the album rather than inward and across the middle. That way they're less likely to be creased or damaged if someone shuts the album without folding the flaps back in.

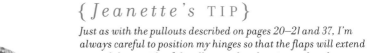

6 Insert page into Memory Protector and position flaps on top of protector. Place cutting mat inside protector behind page, then pierce holes through front of protector and page and attach hinges to page with brads.

PROJECT VARIATION

Spice up your Photo Flaps with all sorts of accents, from brads to buttons to bows. For the *On with the Show* pattern featured in this artwork, turn to page 62.

CUTTING INSTRUCTIONS

B&T Paper

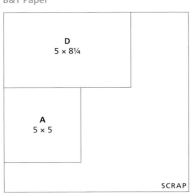

D
5 × 8¼

A
5 × 5

SCRAP

B&T Paper

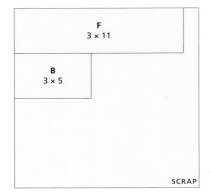

F
3 × 11

B
3 × 5

SCRAP

B&T Paper

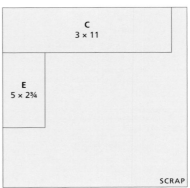

C
3 × 11

E
5 × 2¾

SCRAP

Card Trick™

LAYOUT MATERIALS

12" × 12" Base Cardstock (2)
12" × 12" B&T Paper (3)

PHOTO SUGGESTIONS

1 8" × 6"
2 3" × 2¾" (4)

SUGGESTED TITLE

1 2½" × 6"

SUGGESTED JOURNALING

1 4" × 4¾"

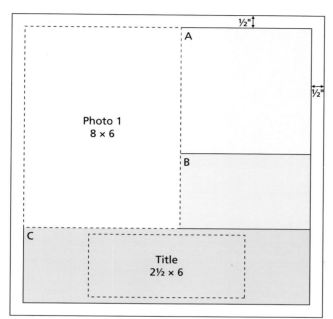

A

Photo 1
8 × 6

B

C

Title
2½ × 6

½"

½"

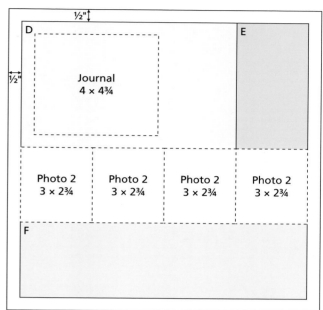

D

Journal
4 × 4¾

E

½"

Photo 2
3 × 2¾

Photo 2
3 × 2¾

Photo 2
3 × 2¾

Photo 2
3 × 2¾

F

½"

LEFT PAGE DIMENSIONS

A 5" × 5"
B 3" × 5"
C 3" × 11"

RIGHT PAGE DIMENSIONS

D 5" × 8¼"
E 5" × 2¾"
F 3" × 11"

{ *Jeanette's* TIP }

Fulfill your wishes to create an original layout by using patterns found in cardmaking how-to books. Just Right, the card pattern used in this artwork, comes from Wishes™, page 39. You can also find this pattern on the enclosed Magic™ DVD.

B&T Paper**

A
11 × 11

SCRAP

B&T Paper**

D
11 × 11

SCRAP

B&T Paper

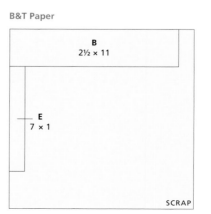

B
2½ × 11

E
7 × 1

SCRAP

Cardstock

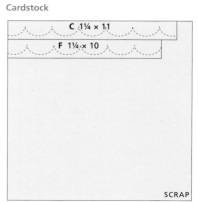

C 1¼ × 11

F 1¼ × 10

SCRAP

**Identical papers

One-Way Mirror™

LAYOUT MATERIALS

12" × 12" Base Cardstock (2)
12" × 12" Cardstock (1)
12" × 12" B&T Paper (3)

PHOTO SUGGESTIONS

1 7" × 5"
2 3½" × 5" (3)

SUGGESTED TITLE

1 2½" × 5½"

SUGGESTED JOURNALING

1 3½" × 5"

* See *One-Way Mirror*
templates on enclosed DVD.

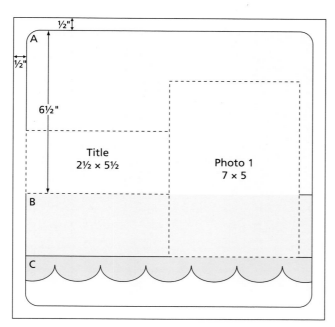

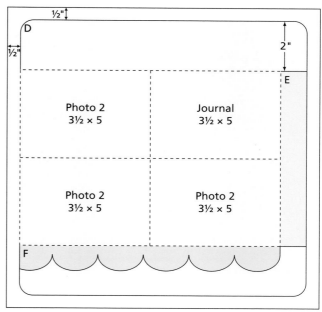

LEFT PAGE DIMENSIONS

A 11" × 11"
B 2½" × 11"
C 1¼" × 11" *

RIGHT PAGE DIMENSIONS

D 11" × 11"
E 7" × 1"
F 1¼" × 10" *

{ *Jeanette's* TIP }

If you want to keep your memories safe and don't have the right size sleeve, create your own by sewing a Memory Protector on three sides and trimming away the excess.

GET 'EM TIGER

B&T Paper

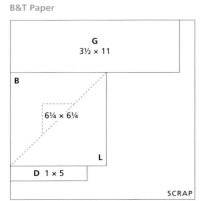

G
3½ × 11

B

6¼ × 6¼

L

D 1 × 5

SCRAP

**Identical papers

B&T Paper

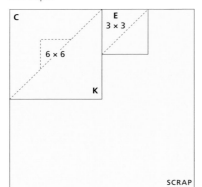

C

E
3 × 3

6 × 6

K

SCRAP

Cardstock**

A
11 × 11

SCRAP

Cardstock**

I
7 × 11

SCRAP

Magic Act™

LAYOUT MATERIALS

12" × 12" Base Cardstock (2)
12" × 12" Cardstock (3)
12" × 12" B&T Paper (2)

PHOTO SUGGESTIONS

1 8" × 10"
2 6" × 4" (2)

SUGGESTED TITLE

1 2½" × 10½"

SUGGESTED JOURNALING

1 1½" × 3½"

* See *Magic Act* templates on enclosed DVD.

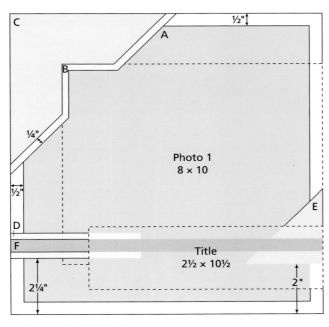

½"
C
A
B
¼"
½"
Photo 1
8 × 10
E
D
F
½"
2¼"
Title
2½ × 10½
2"

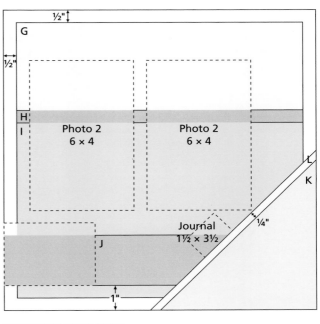

½"
G
½"
H
I
Photo 2
6 × 4
Photo 2
6 × 4
L
K
Journal
1½ × 3½
¼"
J
1"

LEFT PAGE DIMENSIONS

A 11" × 11"
B 6¼" × 6¼" (cut diagonally)*
C 6" × 6" (cut diagonally)*
D 1" × 5"
E 3" × 3" (cut diagonally)
F ½" × 12"

RIGHT PAGE DIMENSIONS

G 3½" × 11"
H ½" × 11"
I 7" × 11"
J 2" × 9"
K 6" × 6" (cut diagonally)
L 6¼" × 6¼" (cut diagonally)

Cardstock

F ½ × 12
H ½ × 11
J
2 × 9
SCRAP

Add a stack of 6" × 4" photos to your layout in record time. It's easy, and your layouts become real page-turners. Turn the page to let the magic begin!

Flip Flaps™

If you have extra photos, Flip Flaps™ are a great way to include them on your layout. These flaps lift open to reveal photos, journaling, or whatever ephemera you'd like to tuck into the 6" × 4" pockets. Layer as many or as few as you like!

STEP-BY-STEP INSTRUCTIONS

1 Insert memorabilia into Flip Flaps™. Layer Flip Flaps directly on top of each other with adhesive strips facing upward, keeping top, right, and left edges flush.

2 Remove backing from adhesive strip of bottom Flip Flap.

3 Attach bottom Flip Flap to corresponding portion of Flip Flap above. Repeat until all Flip Flaps are attached in a stack. *(Note: Top Flip Flap will still have backing on adhesive strip.)*

7 Use hole punch and craft knife to cut slit in Memory Protector along top of Flip Flaps.*

* See page 7 for instructions on cutting Memory Protectors®.

4 Crease Flip Flap stack along score mark beneath adhesive strips, folding back so adhesive portion is hidden behind stack.

8 Reinsert page in Memory Protector, gently working Flip Flaps through slit.

5 Remove backing from adhesive strip of top Flip Flap and attach to page.

{*Jeanette's* TIP}

One way to secure a stack of Flip Flaps™ is to attach ribbon to both the top Flip Flap and the base page, tying them together. Secure a piece of ribbon between two pieces of memorabilia and cut a slit in the Flip Flap to allow the ribbon to slide through. Attach a second piece of ribbon to the base page. Once the Flip Flaps are attached to the page, the two pieces of ribbon can be tied together.

6 Attach remaining photo to page, positioning it directly under the Flip Flaps. Photo will overlap adhesive portion of Flip Flaps.

PROJECT VARIATION

Flip Flaps™ can be placed horizontally or vertically. For the *Raise the Curtain* pattern featured in this artwork, turn to page 66.

B&T Paper

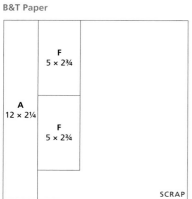

A
12 × 2¼

F
5 × 2¾

F
5 × 2¾

SCRAP

B&T Paper

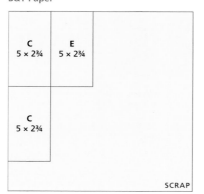

C
5 × 2¾

E
5 × 2¾

C
5 × 2¾

SCRAP

B&T Paper

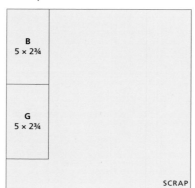

B
5 × 2¾

G
5 × 2¾

SCRAP

Cardstock

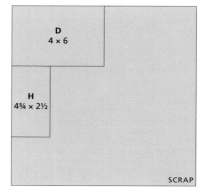

D
4 × 6

H
4¾ × 2½

SCRAP

Illusion™

LAYOUT MATERIALS

12" × 12" Base Cardstock (2)
12" × 12" Cardstock (1)
12" × 12" B&T Paper (3)

PHOTO SUGGESTIONS

1 5" × 5¾" (2)
2 5" × 2¾" (2)

SUGGESTED TITLE

1 3½" × 5½"

SUGGESTED JOURNALING

1 4½" × 2¼"

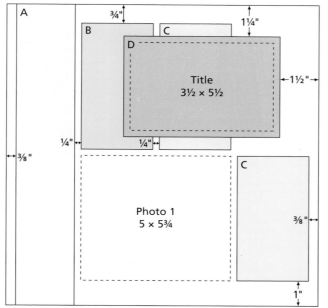

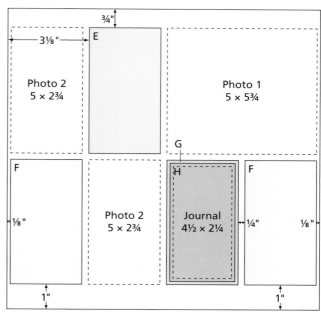

LEFT PAGE DIMENSIONS

A 12" × 2¼"
B 5" × 2¾"
C 5" × 2¾" (2)
D 4" × 6"

RIGHT PAGE DIMENSIONS

E 5" × 2¾"
F 5" × 2¾" (2)
G 5" × 2¾"
H 4¾" × 2½"

{Jeanette's TIP}

Moving elements attached to brads can be slid under fixed elements to create fasteners. On this page, I just slipped the tip of this arrow under the button to hold my hidden journaling shut.

THIS IS
L1FE
ENJOY EVERY MOMENT

Eli, we waited so long for you to be a part of our little
family—how happy we are that you're finally here! You
have a special sweetness about you that is just amazing
to me. You are such a happy, cheerful little soul! Every
day with you is truly a blessing. I can't wait to share
the little moments, and make lots of happy memories with
you!

September
2009

"I'll love you forever,
I'll like you for always,
As long as I'm living
my baby you'll be."
~ Robert Munsch

CUTTING INSTRUCTIONS

B&T Paper

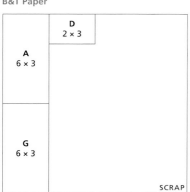

- D 2 × 3
- A 6 × 3
- G 6 × 3
- SCRAP

B&T Paper

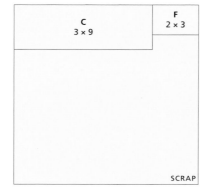

- C 3 × 9
- F 2 × 3
- SCRAP

Cardstock

- B 2 × 3
- E 2 × 3
- SCRAP

Lovely Assistant™

LAYOUT MATERIALS

12" × 12" Base Cardstock (2)
12" × 12" Cardstock (1)
12" × 12" B&T Paper (2)

PHOTO SUGGESTIONS

1 4" × 3" (4)
2 3" × 3"

SUGGESTED TITLE

1 2" × 6"

SUGGESTED JOURNALING

1 4" × 6"

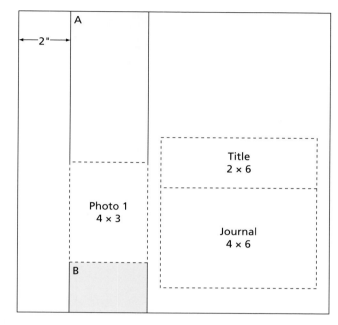

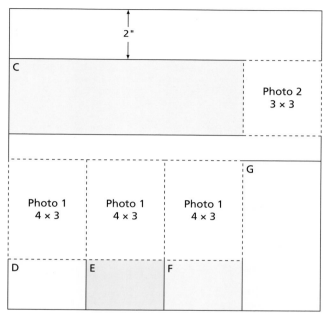

LEFT PAGE DIMENSIONS

A 6" × 3"
B 2" × 3"

RIGHT PAGE DIMENSIONS

C 3" × 9"
D 2" × 3"
E 2" × 3"
F 2" × 3"
G 6" × 3"

· ·

{ *Jeanette's* TIP }

Create your own hinges with ribbon! Attach one end of the ribbon under the fixed piece and the other sandwiched between the two layers of the moving piece. Add as many ribbon hinges as necessary to secure the piece.

B&T Paper

C 8 × 8	
H 3½ × 8	SCRAP

Cardstock

A 5 × 12		
G 5 × 8	**M** 3½ × 3½	
B ½ × 8		
J ½ × 8		SCRAP

Cardstock

E 3½ × 3½	**L** 3½ × 3½	**L** 3½ × 3½
I 2½ × 8	**F** 6 × 6	
K 12 × 1½	**D** 1½ × 8	SCRAP

Abracadabra™

LAYOUT MATERIALS

12" × 12" Base Cardstock (2)
12" × 12" Cardstock (2)
12" × 12" B&T Paper (1)

PHOTO SUGGESTIONS

1 5" × 5"
2 3" × 3" (4)

SUGGESTED TITLE

1 1" × 7½"

SUGGESTED JOURNALING

1 5½" × 3"

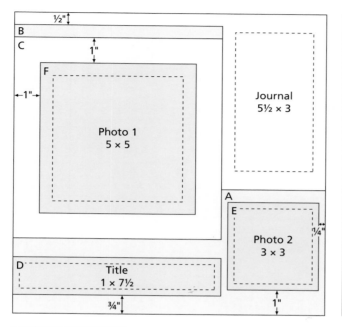

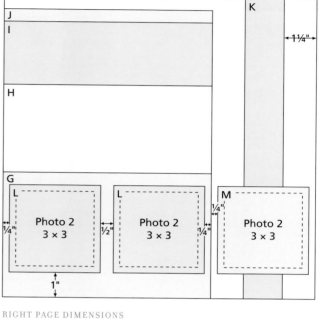

LEFT PAGE DIMENSIONS

A 5" × 12"
B ½" × 8"
C 8" × 8"
D 1½" × 8"
E 3½" × 3½"
F 6" × 6"

RIGHT PAGE DIMENSIONS

G 5" × 8"
H 3½" × 8"
I 2½" × 8"
J ½" × 8"
K 12" × 1½"
L 3½" × 3½" (2)
M 3½" × 3½"

Like a silk scarf pulled from a magician's sleeve, your page just keeps getting bigger . . . and bigger . . . and bigger. Turn the page to let the magic begin!

Go from one page to five in under 60 seconds! Well, it might take you a little more time than that, but it's definitely easy. Whether you purchase pre-made flaps or create your own by sewing Memory Protectors®, this explosive idea is sure to be a favorite. Just attach these oversized flaps to the edges of your page!

FLAP 1: 12" × 8"

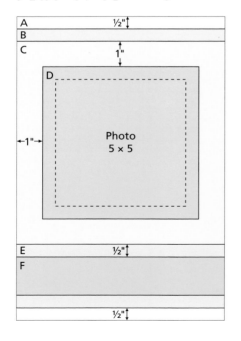

TECHNIQUE MATERIALS

A 12" × 8"
B ½" × 8"
C 8" × 8"
D 6" × 6"
E 2½" × 8"
F 1½" × 8"

PHOTO SUGGESTIONS

1 5" × 5"

FLAP 2: 12" × 4"

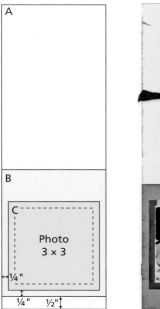

A

B

C

Photo
3 × 3

¼"

¼" ½"

TECHNIQUE MATERIALS

A 12" × 4"
B 5" × 4"
C 3½" × 3½"

PHOTO SUGGESTIONS

1 3" × 3"

FLAP 3: 12" × 4"

A ½"
B
C

D ½"
E

½"

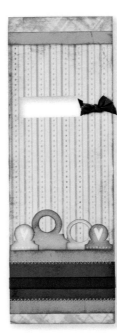

TECHNIQUE MATERIALS

A 12" × 4"
B ½" × 4"
C 8" × 4"
D 2½" × 4"
E 1½" × 4"

the best things
in life are

loving

and being
Loved

FAMILY

{ *Jeanette's* TIPS }

*Use coordinating paper and embellishments for
all of your pieces to make every flap feel cohesive.*

*Attach as few or as many flaps as you like
in order to showcase all your photos.*

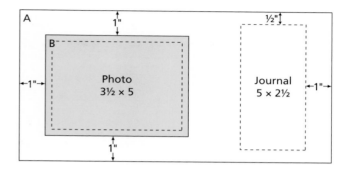

TECHNIQUE MATERIALS

A 6" × 12"
B 4" × 5½"

PHOTO SUGGESTIONS

1 3½" × 5"

SUGGESTED JOURNALING

1 5" × 2½"

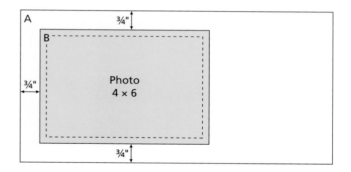

TECHNIQUE MATERIALS

A 6" × 12"
B 4½" × 6½"

PHOTO SUGGESTIONS

1 4" × 6"

Show Stopper

A magician's repertoire should always include a handful of showstoppers: spectacular tricks that make the audience gasp and stare. You can turn any layout into a showstopper, with a little bit of magic. The techniques demonstrated in this section are sure to take your breath away!

CUTTING INSTRUCTIONS

B&T Paper

A 6 × 11	F 11 × 6
	SCRAP

B&T Paper

C 12 × 5½	H 2½ × 12	
		SCRAP

B&T Paper

G
6 × 12

D 12 × ½

SCRAP

Cardstock

B 5 × 11	E 11 × 5	
		SCRAP

106

Showtime™

LAYOUT MATERIALS

12" × 12" Base Cardstock (2)
12" × 12" Cardstock (1)
12" × 12" B&T Paper (3)

PHOTO SUGGESTIONS

1   5" × 7"
2   4" × 4" (5)

SUGGESTED TITLE

1   5½" × 1½"

SUGGESTED JOURNALING

1   6" × 4"

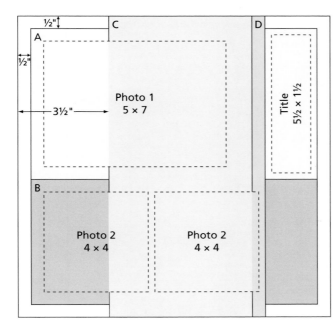

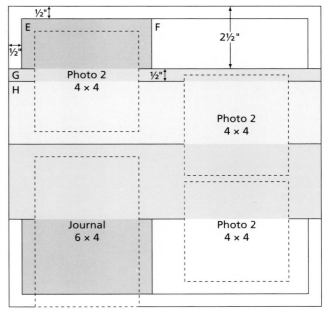

LEFT PAGE DIMENSIONS

A   6" × 11"
B   5" × 11"
C   12" × 5½"
D   12" × ½"

RIGHT PAGE DIMENSIONS

E   11" × 5"
F   11" × 6"
G   6" × 12"
H   2½" × 12"

A photo becomes a bundle of fun when you add flaps that fold out. Turn the page to let the magic begin!

Frame-Up

Even if your mementos are smaller than
5" × 7", the Frame-Up technique gives you a
tidy spot to tuck them away. Add photos to the flaps and decorate
the unused surfaces with stamping and embellishments.

1 Back a photo with
cardstock to create base.
Cut right and left flaps
½" wider than base.

2 Cut top and bottom
flaps ½" taller than base.

3 Score horizontally ½" from bottom of top flap and ½" from top of bottom flap. Score vertically ½" from left edge of right flap and ⅜" from right edge of left flap. Embellish flaps as desired.

5 Fold in each flap to cover center photo. Attach base to page.

4 Attach flaps to back of base, first adhering the top and bottom flaps, followed by the right and left flaps.

6 Use hole punch and craft knife to cut opening in Memory Protector around outside of base.*

* See page 7 for instructions on cutting Memory Protectors®.

{ Jeanette's TIP }

For a tidy stack, fold in the bottom and top flaps first, then the right and left flaps. If you fold them in clockwise (bottom, then left, then top, then right), the edges are a bit difficult to align.

PROJECT VARIATION

The score marks along each flap help the flaps align and can be adjusted as necessary. For the *Abracadabra* pattern featured in this artwork, turn to page 98.

VACATION

SAN FRANCISCO

This was seriously one of the best vacations my husband and I have taken. We traveled with my sister and her husband and spent 3 days together touring the city. We went to the Golden Gate Bridge, saw Lombardi Street, visited Fisherman's Wharf, Ghirardelli Square, and saw Chinatown from the back of a trolley. But one of the best highlights of the trip was seeing Wicked in the opulent Orpheum theatre. I loved every minute of this trip.

B&T Paper

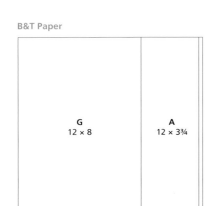

G
12 × 8

A
12 × 3¾

B&T Paper

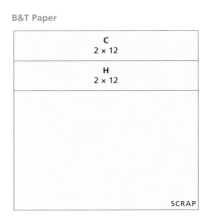

C
2 × 12

H
2 × 12

SCRAP

Cardstock

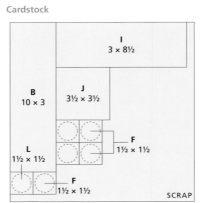

I
3 × 8½

B
10 × 3

J
3½ × 3½

F
1½ × 1½

L
1½ × 1½

F
1½ × 1½

SCRAP

Cardstock

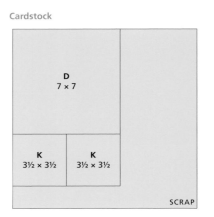

D
7 × 7

K
3½ × 3½

K
3½ × 3½

SCRAP

Juggling Act™

LAYOUT MATERIALS

12" × 12" Base Cardstock (2)
12" × 12" Cardstock (3)
12" × 12" B&T Paper (2)

PHOTO SUGGESTIONS

1 6" × 6"
2 3" × 3" (3)

SUGGESTED TITLE

1 1" × 4"

SUGGESTED JOURNALING

1 2½" × 8"

* See *Juggling Act* template on enclosed DVD.

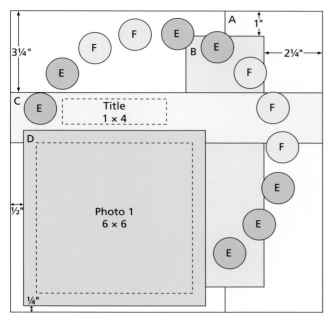

Title
1 × 4

Photo 1
6 × 6

3¼"

2¼"

1"

½"

¼"

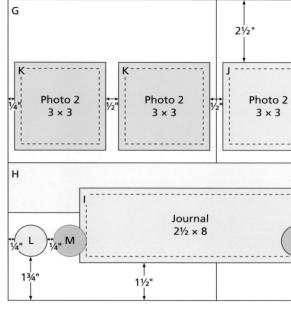

2½"

Photo 2
3 × 3

Photo 2
3 × 3

Photo 2
3 × 3

¼" ½" ½" ¼"

Journal
2½ × 8

¾"

L M   M

¼" ¼"   ¼"

1¾"   1½"   3½"

LEFT PAGE DIMENSIONS

A 12" × 3¾"
B 10" × 3"
C 2" × 12"
D 7" × 7"
E 1¼" Circle (7)*
F 1¼" Circle (5)*

RIGHT PAGE DIMENSIONS

G 12" × 8"
H 2" × 12"
I 3" × 8½"
J 3½" × 3½"
K 3½" × 3½" (2)
L 1¼" Circle*
M 1¼" Circle (2)*

Cardstock

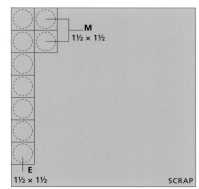

M
1½ × 1½

E
1½ × 1½

SCRAP

{ *Jeanette's* TIPS }

To help you build the Juggling Act layout, I've added a printable circle placement guide to the enclosed DVD.

Hide a photo behind small flaps. Simply cut, score, fold, and add a few photos—it's the perfect way to squeeze in a few more tiny details.

I love it when we take a spontaneous trip together! This quick jaunt to Northern California was just that. We missed your brother, we had a few vacation days on standby, we jumped in the car and we were off! We played tourist by visiting the major sightseeing spots: Golden Gate, Napa Valley, Yosemite and a gorgeous beach. I cherish the time we have together on our little adventures like this. Where do you want to go next?!?

CUTTING INSTRUCTIONS

B&T Paper

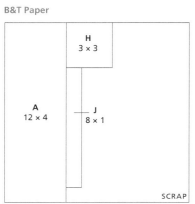

H
3 × 3

A
12 × 4

J
8 × 1

SCRAP

B&T Paper

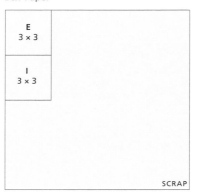

E
3 × 3

I
3 × 3

SCRAP

B&T Paper

K 1 × 8

F 1 × 6

SCRAP

Cardstock

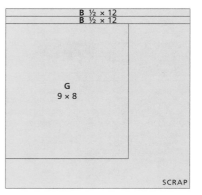

B ½ × 12
B ½ × 12

G
9 × 8

SCRAP

Transfigure™

LAYOUT MATERIALS

12" × 12" Base Cardstock (2)
12" × 12" Cardstock (2)
12" × 12" B&T Paper (3)

PHOTO SUGGESTIONS

1 8" × 6"
2 4" × 3" (2)
3 4" × 6"

SUGGESTED TITLE

1 1¼" × 2½"

SUGGESTED JOURNALING

1 2½" × 2½"

* See *Transfigure* template on enclosed DVD.

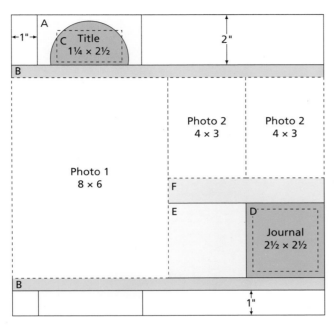
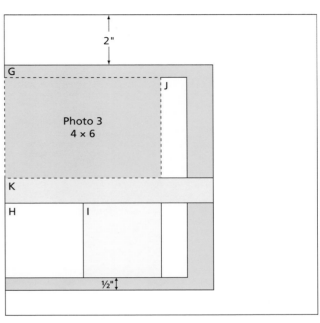

LEFT PAGE DIMENSIONS

A 12" × 4"
B ½" × 12" (2)
C 2" × 3½" *
D 3" × 3"
E 3" × 3"
F 1" × 6"

RIGHT PAGE DIMENSIONS

G 9" × 8"
H 3" × 3"
I 3" × 3"
J 8" × 1"
K 1" × 8"

Cardstock

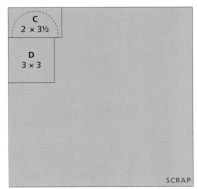

SCRAP

{Jeanette's TIP}

When you create a pouch by popping up a photo or pattern piece, you can use it to hold an entire booklet! Just reinforce the back page of the booklet with cardstock or even chipboard, then slip the back page only into the pocket and let the front pages cover up the pouch.

© 2010 JRL PUBLICATIONS

FUN

FULL SPEED AHEAD

TIMES

B&T Paper

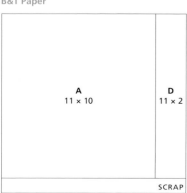

A 11 × 10	**D** 11 × 2
	SCRAP

B&T Paper

B 8 × 11	**E** 11 × 4
	SCRAP

Cardstock

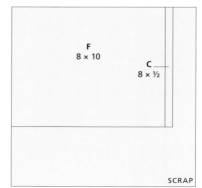

F 8 × 10	**C** 8 × ½
	SCRAP

Top Hat™

LAYOUT MATERIALS

12" × 12" Base Cardstock (2)
12" × 12" Cardstock (1)
12" × 12" B&T Paper (2)

PHOTO SUGGESTIONS

1   3½" × 5" (2)
2   7" × 5" (2)
3   5"× 3½"

SUGGESTED TITLE

1   1¾" × 4½"

SUGGESTED JOURNALING

1   1½" × 3½"

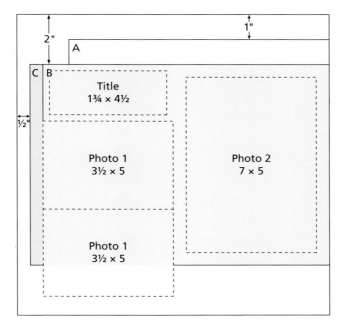

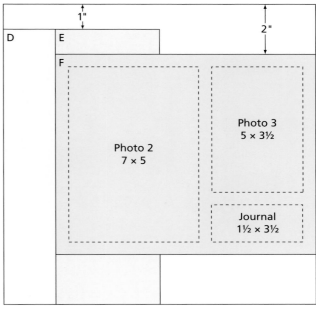

LEFT PAGE DIMENSIONS

A   11" × 10"
B   8" × 11"
C   8" × ½"

RIGHT PAGE DIMENSIONS

D   11" × 2"
E   11" × 4"
F   8" × 10"

{ *Jeanette's* TIP }

A mini album can be more than the sum of its parts. Take a page or two from a mini album and use it to dress up your layout.

B&T Paper

B 3 × 6	**F** 3 × 6

SCRAP

B&T Paper

C 3 × 3	
E 3 × 3	
E 3 × 3	

SCRAP

B&T Paper

G 3 × 3	
G 3 × 3	

SCRAP

Cardstock*

A 11 × 11

SCRAP

*Identical papers

Magician's Choice™

LAYOUT MATERIALS

12" × 12" Base Cardstock (2)
12" × 12" Cardstock (2)
12" × 12" B&T Paper (3)

PHOTO SUGGESTIONS

1 6" × 6"
2 3" × 3" (5)

SUGGESTED TITLE

1 2½" × 5½"

SUGGESTED JOURNALING

1 2½" × 5½"

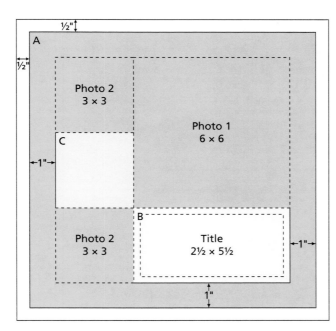

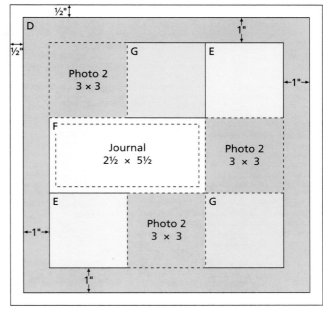

LEFT PAGE DIMENSIONS

A 11" × 11"
B 3" × 6"
C 3" × 3"

RIGHT PAGE DIMENSIONS

D 11" × 11"
E 3" × 3" (2)
F 3" × 6"
G 3" × 3" (2)

Cardstock*

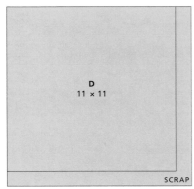

You can stick with the pattern and just attach a piece of Background and Texture (B&T paper), but it's even more fun to create a pretty package containing all sorts of surprises. Turn the page to let the magic begin!

Accordion Booklet

Folding a strip of paper back and forth to make an Accordion Booklet is a breeze. Wrapped up in ribbon, this mini album can be large or small, but it's sure to extend your opportunity to showcase photos and tell your story.

1 Cut two equally sized strips from cardstock. Score vertically at regular intervals on each strip. *(Example: Scored every 3" along each 12" long strip.)*

2 Place strips end to end, overlapping one scored section. Attach to create single long strip.

3 Using center section as base, fold back and forth along score marks to create Accordion Booklet. Embellish as desired.

4 Cut length of ribbon, allowing plenty of ribbon to tie bow around booklet. Attach center of ribbon horizontally to center of booklet base.

5 Tie ribbon in bow on front of booklet and attach booklet base to page.

6 Use hole punch and craft knife to cut opening in Memory Protector around edges of booklet.* Insert page in protector.

* See page 7 for instructions on cutting Memory Protectors®.

{*Jeanette's* TIP}

To keep my Accordion Booklet nice and slim, I use simple and flat decorations inside. I mat photos to help them stand out, and then accent the pages with stamps, ribbon, and cut-outs, rather than thick buttons or brads.

B&T Paper

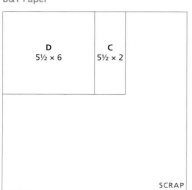

D
5½ × 6

C
5½ × 2

SCRAP

B&T Paper

B ½ × 12

E ½ × 6

F ½ × 4

SCRAP

Cardstock

A
4 × 10

SCRAP

Secret™

LAYOUT MATERIALS

12" × 12" Base Cardstock (2)
12" × 12" Cardstock (1)
12" × 12" B&T Paper (2)

PHOTO SUGGESTIONS

1 5½" × 8"
2 4" × 2½" (4)

SUGGESTED TITLE

1 3" × 8"

SUGGESTED JOURNALING

1 5½" × 4"

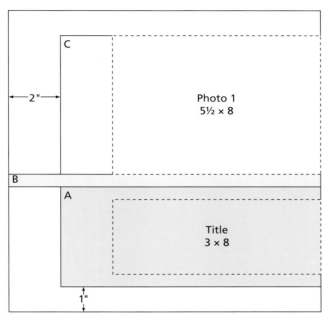

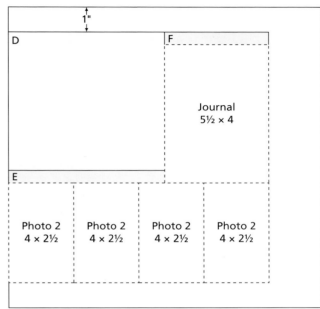

LEFT PAGE DIMENSIONS

A 4" × 10"
B ½" × 12"
C 5½" × 2"

RIGHT PAGE DIMENSIONS

D 5½" × 6"
E ½" × 6"
F ½" × 4"

{ *Jeanette's* TIP }

Notch a pattern piece along the top. Attach sides and bottom only, forming a pocket to hold a CD filled with photos and music guaranteed to bring back memories. You can even decorate the CD with Background and Texture (B&T) paper that matches the rest of your layout!

CLOSE YOUR EYES & MAKE A WISH

One Sunday afternoon we went for a walk. As I watched you picking dandelions and making wishes as you blew them into the breeze, I couldn't help but wonder what you were wishing. And as I watched you making wishes, I made a few wishes of my own. I want you to be healthy and happy. I want you to love and be loved. What I want most is for you to relish every moment in life.

★ '09

CUTTING INSTRUCTIONS

B&T Paper**

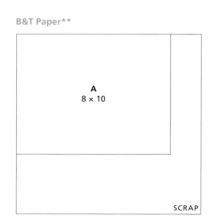

A
8 × 10

SCRAP

**Identical papers

B&T Paper**

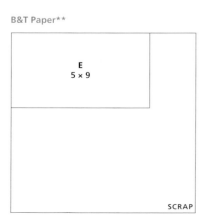

E
5 × 9

SCRAP

Cardstock

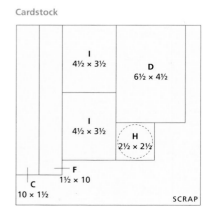

I
4½ × 3½

D
6½ × 4½

I
4½ × 3½

H
2½ × 2½

F
1½ × 10

C
10 × 1½

SCRAP

Cardstock

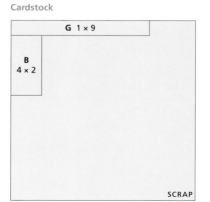

G 1 × 9

B
4 × 2

SCRAP

Final Act™

LAYOUT MATERIALS

12" × 12" Base Cardstock (2)
12" × 12" Cardstock (2)
12" × 12" B&T Duos™ Paper (2)

PHOTO SUGGESTIONS

1 6" × 4"
2 4" × 3" (2)

SUGGESTED TITLE

1 2½" × 6"
2 2½" × 8"

SUGGESTED JOURNALING

1 4" × 3"

* See *Final Act* template on enclosed DVD.

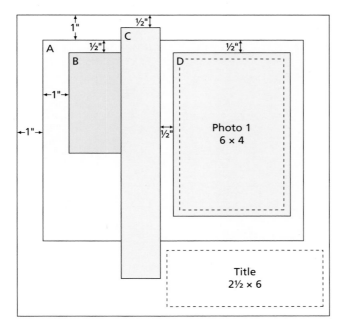

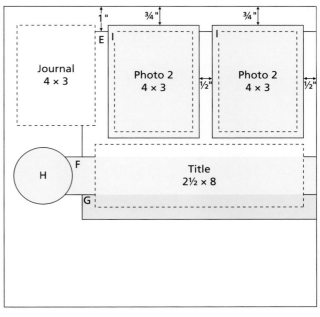

LEFT PAGE DIMENSIONS

A 8" × 10"
B 4" × 2"
C 10" × 1½"
D 6½" × 4½"

RIGHT PAGE DIMENSIONS

E 5" × 9"
F 1½" × 10"
G 1" × 9"
H 2¼" Circle*
I 4½" × 3½" (2)

{ *Jeanette's* TIP }

Replace a focal photo with a stack of tags tied up with a pretty bow. Turn the page to let the magic begin!

Tag Booklet

Pick a tag! Any tag! Like a magician fanning out a deck of cards, when you attach a stack of tags with a brad, you can swivel them out and view each individually. Any tag you pick—we've provided several options here—is sure to be the right one!

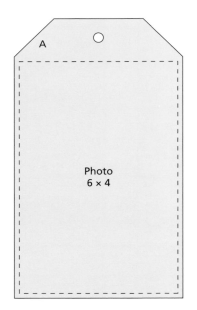

TAG 1

A 7¼" × 4¼"

PHOTO SUGGESTIONS

1 6" × 4"

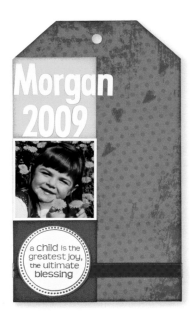

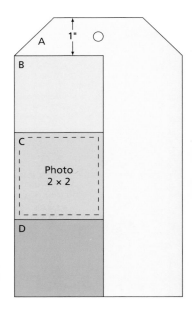

TAG 2

A 7¼" × 4¼"
B 2" × 2¼"
C 2¼" × 2¼"
D 2" × 2¼"

PHOTO SUGGESTIONS

1 2" × 2"

Wish # 1

I wish for you to always take time to stop and smell the flowers. The world is so beautiful. Each day, take time to notice the blue sky, pause to run barefoot through the green grass, stop to listen to the chirping birds. You have a gift for noticing life's little details; I hope that you never lose it. Keep looking for the good in life, and I promise you will find it.

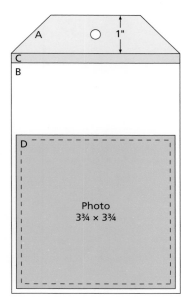

A 1"
C
B
D Photo
3¾ × 3¾

TAG 3

A 7¼" × 4¼"
B 6" × 4¼"
C ¼" × 4¼"
D 4" × 4"

PHOTO SUGGESTIONS

1 3¾" × 3¾"

Wish # 3

I wish for you to remember how much your Heavenly Father loves you. I know that He cares about you very ... hears and ans... I hope that yo... good times ... He'll watch... I hope yo... blessings... You hav...

Wish # 4

I wish for you to make good friends. I now that I may be your best friend now, but that might not always be the case. I hope that you choose friends who see the best in you and encourage you to see the ...

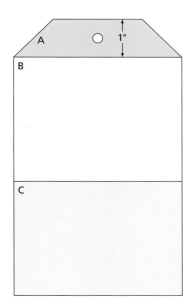

A 1"
B
C

TAG 5

A 7¼" × 4¼"
B 6¼" × 4¼"
C 3" × 4¼" (pocket)

Wish # 2

I wish for you to remember how much I love you. The day you were born, you brought so much light to our little family. You have made us so happy every day since. I don't know that you can ever know how excited we were the day we found out that you were coming. We talked endlessly about what you would look like, and what we should name you. The day finally arrived that you joined our family, and my life has never been the same. I can't imagine a day without you. I love your little giggle, your kissable cheeks, the way you follow me around, and how adorable you are when you're asleep. I love to hear you singing quietly to your dolls as you tuck them in, and that focused look you get on your face while you are coloring with crayons. I love that mischievous little grin that appears when you've been up to something, and even the sound of your voice when you call me "mom," positively melts my heart. Sometimes I just stand in the doorway and watch you, amazed that you are mine to keep forever. You are just growing up too quickly, and I don't want to miss out on anything. So I have to kiss and cuddle with you while you're still little enough to kiss and cuddle back. I hope that even when you get too old for that sort of thing, that you'll still know that I love you more and more each day.

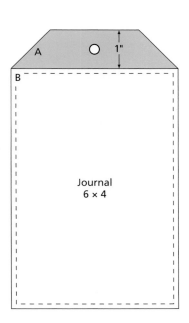

A 1"
B Journal
6 × 4

TAG 4

A 7¼" × 4¼"
B 6¼" × 4¼"

SUGGESTED JOURNALING

1 6" × 4"

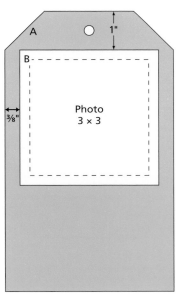

A 1"
B Photo
3 × 3
⅜"

TAG 6

A 7¼" × 4¼"
B 3½" × 3½"

PHOTO SUGGESTIONS

1 3" × 3"

Wish # 5

I wish for you not to grow up too quickly. I hope that you will
relish life, no matter what stage you are in. For some reason, we
have a tendency to want to rush life. We are always looking ahead,
never content with where we are right now. But I hope you treasure
every moment, because you know what? You are going to miss it.
When you are twelve years old, I promise there will be times that
you are going to look forward to sixteen. You will yearn to date and
drive and develop a little more independence. Then when you are
sixteen you will be anxious to be eighteen. You will look forward to
going to college, living on your own, and eventually getting married.
And then, when you are on your own and off at school you will dream
of graduation. When you can have a career or maybe a family and
finally be done with school. But I promise you if you live for
tomorrow, the day will come that you will realize that you missed out
on today. And you will look back at all those times you longed for a
future date and realize that life was pretty wonderful just the way
it was back then. I know that little girls grow up, and I know that
they always grow up faster than their mothers would like them to.
But I also know that life happens soon enough without us rushing on
to the next big thing. I know that to be really happy, you have to
enjoy the moment you are in right now. I hope that the day you do
find that you have "grown up," you will recall with fondness a full
and happy childhood.

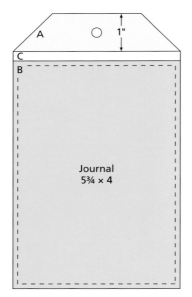

TAG 7

A   7¼" × 4¼"
B   6" × 4¼"
C   ¼" × 4¼"

SUGGESTED JOURNALING

1   5¾" × 4"

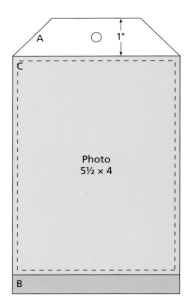

TAG 8

A   7¼" × 4¼"
B   ½" × 4¼"
C   5¾" × 4¼"

PHOTO SUGGESTIONS

1   5½" × 4"

{ *Jeanette's* TIP }

*I've provided patterns for several tags here, but you can mix it up any way
you want. Any combination of tags works! Check out the card patterns in
Originals® and Wishes™ for more inspiration on how to lay out tags.*

PROJECT VARIATION

Put as many tags in your booklet as you
like. The number of tags in your booklet
is only limited by the length of your
brad's prongs! Find tag templates on the
enclosed DVD. For the *Trap Door* pattern
featured in this artwork, see page 76.

Pattern
Index

ALPHABETICAL LISTING

NAME	PAGE	PHOTOS
Abracadabra	98	5
Backstage	28	4
Card Trick	86	5
Charmed	80	5
Crystal Ball	24	5
Deck of Cards	30	5
Disappearing Act	74	4
Enchantment	78	4
Final Act	122	3
Hat Trick	54	3
Hocus Pocus	56	7
Illusion	94	4
Juggling Act	110	4
Levitate	40	4
Love Potion	18	6
Lovely Assistant	96	5
Magic Act	90	3
Magician's Choice	116	6
Mesmerize	34	8
Mystify	36	4
Now You See It	22	4
On with the Show	62	3
One-Way Mirror	88	4
Out of the Hat	82	9
Parlor Trick	14	8
Performance	48	3
Raise the Curtain	66	6
Secret	120	5
Showtime	106	6
Shuffled Deck	42	7
Spellbound	50	6
Ta-Da!	70	4
Top Hat	114	5
Transfigure	112	4
Trap Door	76	3

PHOTO COUNT LISTING

NAME	PAGE	PHOTOS
Out of the Hat	82	9
Mesmerize	34	8
Parlor Trick	14	8
Hocus Pocus	56	7
Shuffled Deck	42	7
Love Potion	18	6
Magician's Choice	116	6
Raise the Curtain	66	6
Showtime	106	6
Spellbound	50	6
Abracadabra	98	5
Card Trick	86	5
Charmed	80	5
Crystal Ball	24	5
Deck of Cards	30	5
Lovely Assistant	96	5
Secret	120	5
Top Hat	114	5
Backstage	28	4
Disappearing Act	74	4
Enchantment	78	4
Illusion	94	4
Juggling Act	110	4
Levitate	40	4
Mystify	36	4
Now You See It	22	4
One-Way Mirror	88	4
Ta-Da!	70	4
Transfigure	112	4
Final Act	122	3
Hat Trick	54	3
Magic Act	90	3
On with the Show	62	3
Performance	48	3
Trap Door	76	3

If you've enjoyed *Magic*, you'll love Jeanette Lynton's other how-to books.
Each one is a must-have for your creative library!
Let Jeanette guide you as you create amazing handmade cards and scrapbook layouts.

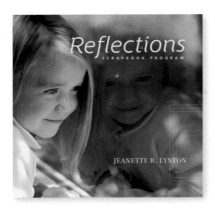

**REFLECTIONS®
SCRAPBOOK PROGRAM**

Unlock your creativity by mixing and matching the 100 single-page patterns in this scrapbook program. Bring your memories to life with ease!

CHERISH™

Patterns, cutting guides, assembly instructions, and tip and technique ideas will help you fashion 50 beautiful two-page scrapbook layouts.

IMAGINE™

Gorgeous scrapbooks are within easy reach! We'll walk you through the process as you create 50 unique two-page layouts to showcase your cherished memories.

**ORIGINALS
CARD CONFIDENCE PROGRAM®**

Success is the only option when you use the step-by-step cardmaking patterns in this book. You'll love the clever techniques we share so you can make each heartfelt card unique!

**WISHES
CARD CONFIDENCE PROGRAM™**

With ten card sizes, trendy circle cards, and three bulk cardmaking workshops, this complete how-to guide will inspire you to create the perfect card for every occasion.

For amazing project ideas, evocative color inspiration,
and fun glimpses into the life of a professional crafter and successful entrepreneur,
follow Jeanette Lynton's blog at

www.jeanettelynton.com